Our Tango World
II: Dancing

Our Tango World II: Dancing

Iona Italia

milonga press

First edition 2019
1 2 3 4 5 6 7 8 9 0

milonga press
England
www.milongapress.com

Paperback: ISBN 978-1-9997551-9-5

Cover design: Nigel Orme

Cover photo: Jeff Topham

Index

At the Milonga

For Eva Karsza, "Foxy," my favourite milonga companion

The Milonga Experience

At its heart, tango is a social dance and what I most love is the crazy Vanity Fair of the milonga, which can be so frustrating when you are sitting rejected on the sidelines; so annoying when people are aggressive or rude; so infuriating to the leaders if the *ronda* degenerates into a clusterfuck. And yet so magical.

We share that space: leaders and followers, men and women, students and teachers, Hungry Boys and Long-Term Beginners. I think I've never felt complete and utter bliss dancing outside that public space. All my best tandas, all my most intense experiences, all my tangasms – were at the milonga. It's our society within a society, the great leveller, where we give and receive the innocent, life-affirming pleasures of our dance. Where we are both naughty and nice and sometimes both at once and receive our presents all the same.

Mirada and Cabeceo

A friend to me: "I believe we could replace most industrial lasers with your *mirada*."

* * *

Cabeceo is basically cruising. That's probably why a friend once sent me a gay video entitled "The Hot Steamy Eye-Fuck" with the remark "this is a *cabeceo* tutorial."

* * *

How to spell cabeceo

A gentle reminder before we begin: it's *CABECEO*. It comes from the word *cabeza* meaning head, not *calabaza*, meaning pumpkin. When you *cabeceo*, use your noddle, not a prize butternut squash. Don't be a pumpkin head. Always spell it *CABECEO*.

Mirada/cabeceo: a guide

—From your seat (at a formal milonga) or from some position from which you have a clear sightline to your target: look at them until you make eye contact. You can do this at any point in the *tanda*, but during the opening bars of the first song is most practical, particularly if the milonga is crowded (later, people on the floor will block your sightlines across the room).

—First, establish eye contact. This may take longer than you think. Be aware that people need time to respond.

—You are both looking at each other? Great. Men (or leaders) indicate your interest in dancing. This is usually done by cocking your head to one side and raising your eyebrows, but choose any gesture that is clear and unambiguous. Women (or followers), nod your agreement.

—If the milonga is very crowded and there are many people seated near you, you might need to clarify that you really are the person intended. Look around to check whether someone next to or behind you is *cabeceoing* your target person. Men (or leaders) might point at their chests and mouth *me?* to clarify.

—Men, if you are sure the woman has accepted, cross the floor and collect her from her seat. Women, stay seated until he gets there, but maintain eye contact with him, smile encouragingly and make bottom-shifting motions to indicate that you are waiting to dance with him.

—Congratulations! Your *cabeceo* was successful.

Some additional considerations:

—Don't *mirada/cabeceo* during the *cortina*. You can, however, do flirtatious pre-*cabeceos*: looking at and smiling at people, so that you know where they are seated and have signalled your probable desire to dance with them at some point in the evening. This is not actually a *cabeceo*, it's more like *hey, cutie pie, I will look for you later*. Like all flirtations, this does not imply any future contractual obligations.

—While there is no rule against dancing consecutive *tandas* with someone, if you have just danced with them within the last couple of *tandas*, they may not be expecting to dance with you again and will probably be unreceptive to your *mirada/cabeceo*.

—If you look over at someone for *mirada/cabeceo* and they wave, grin and mouth 'hello' this usually means "I am acknowledging your eye contact in a friendly way, but I don't want to dance with you right now."

—If someone is seemingly staring fixedly at you but doesn't respond to your gestures, they are probably trying to look at someone directly next to you or behind you. Look away to give them a chance to do that. You can look back at them again later.

—If someone is clearly trying to *cabeceo* someone else, it's fine to wait, see whether they are successful and try to catch their eye if their first choice doesn't work out.

—At milongas where you can move around, don't position yourself really close to your *mirada/cabeceo* target as it can seem very aggressive. Give them the option of graceful refusal.

—Remember that it's fine to have several people in mind for a particular *tanda*. If one *cabeceo* doesn't work, move on to the next. And remember that "no, thanks" in *cabeceo* means "not right now" not necessarily "no, never."

—What happens if someone is trying to *mirada/cabeceo* you and you *don't* want to dance with them? Just look away. Maybe flash them a smile as you let your gaze wander elsewhere. There is no need to avoid eye contact altogether. Making eye contact with someone is not in itself a *cabeceo*. Both parties have to also make a head gesture to signal their agreement to dance. Don't shake your head or mouth "no, thanks" or, even worse, wag a disapproving finger at them. That's overkill—to most people it signals "I will *never* dance with you!" And it could be misunderstood by others around who might think the statement is meant for them.

—Final point: what happens if I make a mistake? If you make a mistake, you will be publicly flogged.

Not.

It can easily happen that two men cross the floor, both thinking their *cabeceo* has been accepted by the same woman. As women usually stay seated, our mistakes are less obvious, but often two women think they have been accepted by the same man. If this happens, it really is no big deal. There is no obligation to dance with the person who was mistaken about the object of the *cabeceo*, either immediately or in the future. The people who actually wanted to dance with each other, go ahead and dance, after a brief apology to the *mistakees* (as I'll call them). If you were the one who was confused, don't worry. It happens to everyone from time to time and is no reason for any special drama.

The Semaphore Mirada/Cabeceo

To successfully *mirada* or *cabeceo* someone who is sitting at the very opposite end of a large room or to do so in low-light conditions or when your eyesight isn't 20-20 requires a little skill. I recommend the mirroring approach.

First, look at your target for longer than you might think necessary. Don't get distracted by the sea of eyes looking back out at you, don't let your gaze turn blurry and wander, but focus very clearly on one single person. The further they are away from you, the more intently you should stare (this does not have the same aggressive effect as it would close up). It doesn't matter if you can't see the exact expression in their eyes: you don't have to lip read; it's all about lines and directions.

4

Women, if he wants to dance with you, he will probably cock his head to one side. If you nod in agreement and he still looks puzzled, cock your head too.

If you can't see well enough to tell whether someone is looking directly into your eyes, then men (or leaders) try making a really big gesture, such as tilting your whole body to one side. Make it almost comically exaggerated and see if she copies you (it will be quite intuitive). Women, if you can see the man's gesture but not his eyes, do the same thing. Mirror it back to him. Exaggerate a little. Does he respond by repeating it back to you? You're on to a good thing.

If someone you often dance with seems to be craning their neck in your direction, make some actions as if you were craning *your* neck or moving your head to one side, around an invisible obstacle or over the top of an imaginary head. (Be very careful not to obstruct other people's sightlines as you do this.)

Women, the leader might still not know that you are definitely asking *him* to dance – and remember that the man is the one who will have to get up and cross the floor to collect you from your chair, so he will naturally be wary of approaching in case you are actually trying to *mirada* someone else.

Men, point at your chest and mouth "*yo? ('me?')*." Women, point straight at him (from this distance it isn't rude) and lip synch "*vos!*" (*'you!'*), nodding vigorously. Men, you can try shifting your head from one side to the other, looking at the woman from left and right. Women, mirror him. You'll find there is a few seconds' pause and then, with a final finger pointing to his chest and eyebrows raised in query (nod like one of those felt dogs on a Ford Cortina dashboard in response) he will get up and start walking towards you.

Maintain eye contact with each other as the leader approaches. But women, don't leap out of your chair – sometimes you'll find that a woman next to or behind you was the intended recipient of his mime and you were an unknowing copycat, an innocent eavesdropper on their non-verbal conversation. But if he has got all the way to your chair and is standing there in front of you, congratulations to both of you.

Mirada cruising can also be an excellent strategy at a large venue (such as a festival) where you have the freedom to move around the room. Wander around and discreetly set up some good sight lines for yourself. It's a bit like bird watching. If you get too close, you will spook them. (Sometimes, you may have to move further away to get a good purchase on your target). Going right up to the person and staring at them from six inches away is creepy. But sometimes you do need to employ your special sniper *mirada* and send some extra-intense eye-lasers out from a medium distance. Men, resist the temptation to go up to the woman and ask her verbally at her table: this is not always well received (see below).

If this all sounds very complicated, remember this: a lot of people at crowded milongas dance all night long, with a slew of different partners. There are many successful ocular transactions happening all the time, often at what seems like lightning speed, without a word having been spoken (watch how quickly the floor flushes full as the *tanda* begins, as if someone had opened the gates of a human sluice – even though we have many myopic glasses-wearers here). You might need a little practice, but this is a system which has evolved because it's quick, efficient and easy.

A follower's ocular strategies

One of the cultural misunderstandings which arises when dancers are unfamiliar with *mirada/cabeceo* is that men don't realise that it's possible for women to be proactive in their choices, by using their eyes to signal who they wish to dance with. As I sat in the Cuban bar in Miami one evening, I was employing those peepers diligently because I am accustomed to selecting my partners (though, of course, they always have to choose me, too).

For the first couple of *tandas* I watched the floor attentively, deciding whose dancing I liked the look of. Out of the corner of my eye, I sometimes noticed guys getting up and preparing to walk over to ask me (to be welcoming to the new person, perhaps, or chivalrous) and looked away demonstratively, hoping that that would save them a verbal rejection. But the guys were completely unaccustomed to reading body language; they were surprised by my polite "no, thanks" (especially since I was clearly eager to dance). They were oblivious to the idea that a woman could signal, with looks and gestures, her wish to dance with a man – or not. I felt a little awkward as I declined four drive-by verbals in a row.

Meanwhile, I spotted a tall older guy dressed in head-to-toe black who seemed to be dancing a creative and musical *salón*. "Have you danced with him?" I asked a female neighbour and when she said she hadn't, I offered to test the waters for her in my rickety little craft, like a royal taster sampling a dish for her monarch. As the new *tanda* began, I looked firmly and clearly over in his direction and with an economical inclination of his head and a nod of mine, we were on (as a reader once put it, "*Accio* broomstick; let's fly!").

Later, I was sitting next to a friend, keeping him in my peripheral vision, as we both sat peacefully observing the floor, watching to see whether his eyes strayed over towards mine as the *tanda* of Troilo milongas began. And later, cheekily, I switched positions to a different couch for a sightline to a difficult quarry, got the DJ in my crosshairs and snipered him with a bold look. *Bang bang! I shot him down!* He was delicious.

When someone comes up and asks me to dance, they catch me by surprise. I haven't chosen them. Usually there is a moment of bewilderment and then, mostly, I say "no, thanks." Because I don't know what would await me on the dance floor and the fact that he asked me verbally is, in itself, generally a bad sign (more experienced dancers usually use *cabeceo*). In addition, I want to support other women's ability to say "no, thanks" to unwanted dances by doing so myself. As Tine Herreman memorably puts it, *bitches afford protection*.

Many guys ask women to dance verbally as a polite gesture. Some may even feel obligated. Because they think that we are sitting there demurely waiting to be asked, flowers for the plucking. But, actually, many of us are very actively selecting our partners.

Well, I certainly am and I'd encourage other women to do the same. I don't get to dance with everyone I'd like to. But I get to *choose*.

Approaching the table

At some Buenos Aires milongas, such as *Salón Canning*, many women get offended if a man asks them to dance verbally by coming up to their table. Why?

This is partly because it is intrinsically problematic when someone asks you to dance, sight unseen. If *Mr Stranger Man* is looking over in my direction and he is an unknown quantity, I can discreetly look away, without offending him. Then, if I see him dancing later and it looks appealing, I can try to catch his eye and, this time, accept his *cabeceo* if he offers. However, if *Mr Stranger Man* comes to my table to ask me to dance, I will probably say "no, thanks" because I am risk averse. That may feel awkward, especially if I am turning him down in front of my friends or, worse, his. And if he turns out to be a good dancer, I may have missed my chance; he probably won't ask me again.

At places like *Canning*, it tends to be only the less experienced dancers who ask women to dance at their tables. Many women choose those places specifically *because* they do not like being asked to dance verbally. So the very fact that a leader is asking that way tends to prejudice the women against him. My advice to leaders at such places is to wear a really nice suit (looking the part won't hurt), get within optimum *cabeceo* distance of your chosen victim and then use *cabeceo*. Don't approach the table.

Hovering over someone isn't cabeceo

Walking over to someone, standing right in front of their chair and staring intensely at them at point blank range is not a *cabeceo*. If they cannot avoid your gaze except by looking straight down at the floor and cannot see anything past you when they look up, it's not a *cabeceo*. If you are standing over them in a way which would make someone trying to read small print, sew or apply mascara ask you to move because you were blocking their light, you're too close. It doesn't matter whether you are stiller than a pillar of salt and more silent than me when I'm trying to remember the punch line of a joke. Looming over someone is not *cabeceo*. Full stop.

Just looking at someone isn't a cabeceo

Just looking at a woman isn't a *cabeceo*. No matter how longingly you gaze, nothing is going to happen unless you make a clear gesture. You can tilt your head, raise your eyebrows, or do a chin jut or inquiring nod – whatever signals a visible and obvious invitation.

And, women, remember that eye contact alone is not a *mirada/cabeceo*. You both look at each other, he (usually) tips his head and you nod to accept. It's a little two-sided mime.

You should probably avoid gazing at people for hours without making any kind of gesture. They might find it flattering or creepy, but it probably won't work as a way of requesting a dance.

Cabeceo triage

In some scenes, *mirada/cabeceo* acts as a code which more experienced dancers use to identify each other. Tine Herreman describes this as "the *cabeceo* triage."

I'm repeatedly told that dancers in community x "don't use *mirada/cabeceo*" only to find a small subgroup of the dancers using it extensively and receive most of my dance invitations that way.

Mirada/cabeceo requires the cooperation of both parties and perhaps in your community the people you would like to dance with aren't interested in using it. But take a good, careful look around before you assume that *no one* is using it or that it's *impossible* to use in your local tango scene.

Mirada/cabeceo and plausible deniability

People you enjoy dancing with are a very precious resource so it's important not to squander those opportunities for pleasure. People you don't currently enjoy can grow and develop. Their dance can change and so can yours, making you more suitable partners for each other. So it's important not to shrink your potential pool of partners for the future. *Mirada* and *cabeceo* provide a cover of plausible deniability. You don't have to decide, once and for all, whether to dance with someone. The practice lessens the possibility of taking offence at someone not dancing at you that particular evening and makes it less feasible to say "you deliberately and specifically rejected *me*."

The lack of verbal communication causes some mysteries and heartaches – why does he no longer respond to my *mirada*? why is she avoiding my *cabeceo*? – but it also allows for the possibility of future developments. You can choose not to dance with someone right now *without* committing to never dancing with them. And vice versa: you can dance with them without a fear that this implies future obligations. As John Major used to say, you're not ruling anything out and you're not ruling anything in.

People who ignore your ocular invitations to dance.

Here in Baires, many people are in the habit of strategizing their partner choices. Many people dance only one *tanda* per partner per night.

So here's what frequently happens: a beautiful Troilo-Fiorentino *tanda* is sounding. I know *Flirty Boy* often dances Troilo with me, so I cast my eyes in his direction, hopefully. But his gaze slides past mine blankly or he looks fixedly at a different corner of the room. What's happening? Am I being rejected?

No. It's just that he wants to dance with that French lady who always leaves early (he knows I stay till the end). Or his girlfriend is here and he's saving the especially intense *tandas* for her. Or that girl he's been wanting to dance with *finally* looks as though she might be eyeing him invitingly. Or his friend just nudged him: "hey that Japanese woman is looking at you. I just danced with her; she's great." Or he knows the velvety intensity of Troilo-Marino will be up later and *then* we will have our *tanda*. He hasn't cancelled our nightly rendezvous. It's just been scheduled for later.

Mirada/cabeceo relies on serendipity. You can only arrange to dance when you are both looking at each other at the same moment. That one instant can change someone from the cool customer playing hard to get to the eager playmate. Every *tanda* is a new roll of the dice, an opportunity for new pairings.

The same is true of every milonga. You might not dance tonight, but perhaps tomorrow, next week, next month or next year. Perhaps not until one or both of you has changed your dance in certain ways. Because, as dancers, we don't stay the same. Serious dancers are always studying and conscious study leads to changes that affect who we are compatible with on the floor.

In *mirada/cabeceo*, people avoid a direct statement of rejection. "Would you like to dance with me?" is a yes/no question. By using *mirada/cabeceo*, we avoid the question, we don't pin ourselves down, we leave the possibility of dancing open for later: for another *tanda*, another night or another time.

For this to work, you need open-mindedness, patience and calm. You need to wait for the right person at the right moment. Just like in life.

When you only have your eyes to work with, it's much harder to force, coerce, pressurise, guilt trip, schmooze or shame someone into dancing with you.

You can't stand next to a man making small talk and flirting and then hang around, batting your eyelashes, sneaking little glances at him and waiting for him to ask you to dance out of politeness or to escape from an awkward situation.

You can't go up to a person and say "please dance with me, I haven't danced all evening"; "I've always admired your dancing, please dance with me"; "I'm not a very good dancer, but dance with me anyway" or "if you dance with me, I might take private lessons from you."

You can't make a big drama out of striding diagonally across the floor, hand outstretched, confidently trusting that the woman will say yes because she is too polite to make you look bad in front of her friends.

You can't deliberately plant yourself in front of someone, blocking their lines of sight or obscuring them from the gaze of others in the hopes that they will dance with you just to rid themselves of a nuisance.

You can't sit next to them, despite their obvious discomfort, making them feel embarrassed to look past you to dance with someone else and obliged, out of kindness, to dance with you first.

You can't demand reasons why they don't want to dance with you, insult them or start an argument about it.

You can't whine, cajole, threaten or beg.

You can't try to coerce them into a dance even if they aren't looking in your direction, are deep in conversation, are attempting to make eye contact with someone else or have been avoiding you all evening.

You can't follow them around the room, hold a stakeout in front of the toilets, stalk them from chair to chair or 'playfully' tug them out onto the floor so that they have to put up an embarrassing struggle to free themselves.

In short: you can't dance with someone who doesn't want to dance with you. You can't try to convince them with words, use words to question their decision or bully them if they decline. You're only able to dance with those who look straight at you, respond to your signals and demonstrate their willingness. You can't attempt to force a dance.

Perhaps you don't do those things when you ask someone to dance verbally anyway. I hope not. But, in a *mirada/cabeceo* only environment, *no one* does those things because they can't.

The Supertanguera and her mirada superpower

There are two approaches to partner choice in tango. There are those who ask only "do I want to dance right now?" and "do I think I would like dancing with this person who is looking my way?"

The second approach involves a much more complicated mental flowchart with boxes that say "Have I danced with her already this week? How many *tandas*? How many other people would I still like to dance with? Am I in the mood for his way of dancing? Might I have a chance of getting a dance with someone more desirable if I decline this one? Am I too tired to do it justice? Should I have had that second margarita? Perhaps I should dance with X instead who is easier to dance with? Wouldn't I really prefer to dance this D'Arienzo *tanda* with Y?" For some, accepting or declining a dance is a split-second decision taken in the moment and others have a (sometimes inscrutable) master plan.

But there are some women whose dancing is so wonderful that it has given them the tango superpower, The Invincible *Mirada*. The leader can be limping to the toilet with a bursting bladder and a twisted ankle as the DJ spins a *tanda* of alternative speed metal-rap-tango fusion and such a woman can stop him in his tracks and make him come back and embrace her. The leader can be slumped in a chair, legs spread, eyelids just flickering closed and then suddenly "oh my God, *she* is looking at me. Must. Dance. *KABOOM!*" They are very few of these superheroines, but they are out there.

That's my new motivation for practising. I want to go into a public phone booth, spin around fast and come out with a cape billowing around my shoulders, wearing my underwear on top of my tights. I want to be a *Supertanguera*.

When cabeceo 'isn't working'

"I know I should use *cabeceo* here, but I can't catch your eye. You keep looking away. So I had to come over and ask you." If you find yourself saying this to someone – just stop for a moment and think about it. Maybe your *cabeceo* is working perfectly. Just not in the way you'd like.

Schmoozeceo

In many places outside Buenos Aires, the main method for getting dances for women is as follows. Go up to a man with whom you have some slight acquaintance, hang around next to him, make chit chat, pretend to be interested in what he is saying and wait for him to ask you to dance. Of course, in some cases, people are just genuinely enjoying conversation with each other. But I have often heard the advice that to dance with a guy you need to 'butter him up.' I often see the guys talking and the women standing looking very obviously impatient and bored, as they don't *really* want to chat, they are just waiting to be asked to dance. I can tell from their twitchy body language and their eyes flicking suggestively towards the dance floor at every pause in the discourse.

This is clearly a strategy that has evolved in many tango scenes, though in Buenos Aires, it is less effective, since people here generally separate friendliness towards someone from dancing with them. But I feel very uncomfortable with *schmoozeceo*: because of the passive position it puts the women in and the way it makes social interactions seem fake.

Asking people to dance verbally: some don'ts

If you want to ask a woman (or man) to dance verbally and increase your chances of her (or him) accepting, here are some things you should *not* do.

1. Don't come up and ask during the *cortina*. (It looks as though you don't care what music you dance to – not a good thing).

2. Don't walk straight across the dance floor mid-song. When people do this, I find it quite astonishing – and not in a good way.

3. If, as you start approaching, s/he suddenly develops an intense fascination with the floor, her mobile phone or a spider's web on the ceiling in the opposite corner of the room and/or turns her whole body away from you – don't go up and tap her on the shoulder.

4. Don't preface your request with "I can't get you to look at me, so I've been forced to come over and get you." If someone is avoiding looking at you, it's usually for good reason.

In the event that you hear a polite "no, thanks":

1. Don't sit down right next to him or her immediately after s/he has declined to dance with you.

2. Don't ask why she declined to dance with you: "Oh, are you a non-dancer?" "Are you resting this *tanda*?" "Do your feet hurt, then?" and other questions are really inappropriate.

3. Don't snort, scoff, shrug your shoulders or show other gestures of anger. And definitely don't say "well be like that then."

How to ask a man to dance

I am always asking men to dance – with my eyes. I'm skilled at using my peepers. And I love the *mirada/cabeceo* system because it's egalitarian (we *both* ask each other to dance; it's a two-way mime).

It isn't the optimum solution under every conceivable circumstance. Sometimes, at more informal places or among friends, it's fine to ask each other to dance verbally. Under those circumstances, it's just as appropriate for women to ask men to dance as vice versa. The only argument to the contrary is that it is the man who usually leads and leading involves dealing with the conditions on the floor. There may be situations in which an inexperienced leader is tempted by the idea of dancing with a desirable follower or doesn't want to hurt a friend's feelings and therefore ventures out onto a *pista* which is too hectic or crowded for him to safely negotiate. If you're asking a leader to dance, you should bear that in mind.

Try to follow a few common sense guidelines when asking. First, the less awkward it is to approach the person, the more likely your chances of success. If the man in question looks exhausted or is fanning himself and dripping saltily onto the floor, you should probably refrain. If he's chatting, especially to another woman, you probably shouldn't approach. Don't rush over to someone distant.

And if you have to touch the person to get their attention, it's probably not a good idea to ask (unless they are a close friend).

But if a guy is hovering by the edge of the dance floor, looking out, moving to the music and occasionally glancing around hopefully and if he seems like a relaxed person – especially if he looks like a newcomer to the local scene – I may ask him to dance. I also ask close friends with whom I've often danced. And I frequently ask women leaders to dance. Since not everyone is comfortable dancing with someone of their own sex, they might not otherwise know that I would be happy to be led by them.

As for other men witnessing the interchange and disapproving, I believe those fears are largely unfounded, at least at informal milongas (please don't go up and ask people to dance at a milonga where *mirada/cabeceo* is clearly the overwhelming norm – observe what the locals are doing before you act). You cannot second guess everyone's reaction, but, over the years, I have not noticed any sanctions being placed on women who ask men to dance. It is true that many Argentine women, at the most informal milongas, sit quietly waiting for guys to come over and ask them. But I personally don't feel comfortable being placed in such a passive position.

How do I ask? I recommend the least complicated way possible. Keep it light and low key. The less you say, the better – it's easier for the other person to refuse if it does not seem like a big deal. I usually just say the single word "*Bailás?*" ("Want to dance?")

Of course, if you ask someone to dance, you need to be prepared to hear a polite refusal. This is a good thing. Being able to accept refusals with grace is a vital skill in all areas of life.

What a refusal might mean

(1) I'm tired or injured, so, just for tonight, I'm only dancing with reliable old favourite partners who I know will treat me gently.

(2) I'm a little tipsy and I don't mind dancing with close friends (who won't judge) but I'm not going to inflict my wobbly self on a stranger (*especially* if he/she is a good dancer).

(3) I haven't had a chance to see you dance and I don't feel like risking a *tanda* with any more unknowns tonight.

(4) You're a beginner and I want to encourage you – but I've danced with my quota of inexperienced partners tonight. We'll dance next time.

(5) You have Left Arm Issues and my right arm is already a little achy from dancing with cyborg leaders with iron arms. I love your musicality. But I've got to let my arm muscles recover before I embrace you. (This reason is more frequently applicable than you might think).

(6) I'm not crazy about this orchestra but I will dance to it if *Dreamboat cabeceos* me because he is too tempting to miss out on ever.

(7) I love dancing with you, but I ESPECIALLY enjoy it to Di Sarli (you're so gorgeously smooth). You tend to dance only one *tanda* with me per evening, so if I dance these bouncy Biagis with you, I'll miss out on the opportunity to glide around the floor with you to *El cielo y tú*.

(8) This is very big, dramatic music. I'm waiting for a set of simple Canaros to look in your direction. Your dancing is nice when the intense music doesn't tempt you to camp it up.

(9) I'd love to dance with you later, but right now *Dreamboat* is finally looking at me. I'm not taking my eyes off him till I see whether he's about to give me his characteristic tilted *cabeceo*.

(10) This is my favourite orchestra. It's special to me and I'm extra choosy about who I dance it with. Catch me later, for a different band.

How to decline dances gracefully

I try to separate being friendly and sociable from accepting or declining dances and to be as polite towards those I don't want to dance with as those I do. I don't deliberately snub, ignore or avoid all eye contact with someone, in order to deter him (or her) from asking me to dance.

If I want to turn down a *cabeceo*, I just look away or don't react. If someone makes a verbal request that I want to turn down, I almost always say a simple "no, thanks." In the unusual event of them asking for an explanation, I can be quite stubborn in refusing to give one.

I do give explanations sometimes: if the person asking is a friend I genuinely want to dance with, but can't right at that moment ("sorry, I promised this *tanda* to X"; "actually, I was about to go because I need to get up early tomorrow"; "I'm not crazy about this music; let's wait for the next *tanda*") or if they announce to me that they are a beginner ("I think this floor is a bit challenging, but I'll happily dance with you when it's not as busy"; or "sure, but let's dance later, to less dramatic music.") Otherwise, I find it best not to give any explanations or excuses.

I try to be friendly, regretful and undramatic in the way I say "no, thanks": like a dieter refusing a slice of delicious cake, not like someone declining to buy polyester knock-off Adidas socks from a panhandler.

Of course, people can always read things you never intended into a look or tone of voice. Rejections are awkward by nature. If you decline dances, you will hurt some people's feelings, upset some and may even anger a few. In some communities, you might even be labelled a bitch or a snob (though the better dancers are highly unlikely to hold that against you).

But, personally, I find it almost impossible to dance with people I suspect or know I won't enjoy dancing with. Dancing is an intense, focused experience. I can't bring myself to just go through the motions to be polite. Like kissing, I love it, but not with everyone. So, while saying "no, thanks" is difficult, it's worth doing. And it's worth learning to do it as graciously as you can manage.

Passive rejections

If, in your scene, the men do most or all of the asking to dance, you might get the false impression that women have all the power and choice in tango. In fact, women get rejected all the time: when they are longing to dance with a man and he *doesn't* look in their direction to *cabeceo* them and *doesn't* ask them to dance. These rejections may be invisible, but they are real.

In many tango scenes, women face a double whammy of disadvantage. On the one hand, if there is a strong gender imbalance, they usually get to dance much less than they would like. This almost inevitably means that they suffer more rejections and disappointments than the men. And, in addition, if the men walk over to ask them verbally, they may face social pressures to say yes to dances that they *don't* want. So the women often suffer on two fronts:

they don't get the dances they would like *and* are under pressure to accept dances that they don't want.

That's why I believe in *mirada/cabeceo*, in which both parties are active; why I believe that if men ask women to dance verbally, it should be equally acceptable for women to ask men; why I advocate discretion when asking someone to dance; why I don't believe in the 'penalty box'; and why I fiercely defend the rights of both sexes to free partner choice. Rejection can hurt − for both men and women *equally*. And we both have to learn to deal with it graciously.

The penalty box

The so-called "penalty box" rule supposedly stipulates that if a man asks a woman to dance verbally and she says "no, thanks," she should sit out that *tanda*. The rule is also sometimes applied to women asking men or to same-sex partners.

We, all of us, need to learn to take rejections gracefully. No *tanda* belongs to us by right and we cannot hold anyone else to ransom. When you ask someone "would you like to dance?" you are really asking "would you like to dance this *tanda* now, *with me?*" not "do you enjoy dancing in general?" There could be many reasons why the person would not like to dance with you. Any and all of those reasons could be perfectly valid.

This also means that the person doing the rejecting has to take responsibility and say a simple "no, thanks" if they don't wish to dance. I know it's tempting, but it's best not to offer white lies or excuses such as "my feet hurt" or "I don't like this orchestra," unless you really are prepared to forgo dancing that *tanda*. It's impolite to say you're "resting" and then leap up to dance the *tanda* with someone else.

The notion of the penalty box encourages entitlement, possessiveness, envy and resentment. We can't avoid *having* those feelings. But we can avoid creating codes which valorise them.

More Milonga Etiquette Advice

Terpsi's Tango Etiquette Rules

1. However I ask for dances (almost always by *mirada*), I try to do so in a way that leaves room for a graceful refusal.

2. I don't get my knickers in a twist because someone declines to dance with me, whether stranger, teacher, student, friend, host, beginner, expert, etc. I might be disappointed, but I don't get angry. I separate friendships from dance relationships. We can be friends, even if you don't like dancing with me, or vice versa.

3. I generally break *tanda* for bad behaviour, not bad dancing, unless dangerous driving and/or actual pain or danger of bodily injury is involved.

4. If I don't want to dance with someone, I say "no, thank you." I don't offer explanations or excuses unless these are genuine. And I feel free to dance with someone else for that *tanda*.

5. I shower before the milonga, wear my strongest deodorant and brush my teeth.

6. I don't teach people on the dance floor.

7. I tip waiters (and flirt with them), recommend teachers, greet organisers, compliment other women on their clothes and dancing and point out if a good dancer is trying to catch a friend's eye for *cabeceo* (conversely, I warn against disastrous dancers).

8. I wish performers "*mierda*," applaud performances and, if I didn't like them, avoid commenting and remain diplomatic if my opinion is solicited.

9. I don't get jealous if my boyfriend really loves dancing with another woman and I expect complete freedom to dance with whoever I want, even when I'm in a relationship.

Teaching at the milonga

I don't dance with someone in order to learn from them, practise on them, copy or emulate them, or get used to a particular style of leading. I don't do it to teach them either – to critique them, model good dancing for them or correct them. There are times and places for teaching and learning and the milonga is not one of them.

Of course, you *can* learn things at the milonga. But it's incidental learning. Real practice takes place elsewhere: at the *práctica*, in lessons, at home, in the practice room. At the milonga, I don't want to give or receive technical feedback; I don't want them to practise certain moves on me. I want to focus on being in the music and with my partner and trust my body to do the things I've trained it to – imperfectly, but without conscious monitoring.

It's important to have a space where tango is pure play, a place consecrated to pleasure. It's neither selfish nor egotistical to want to play there. Most of us have, frankly, enough work-related stress in the rest of our lives. A happy person who gets their tango playtime is usually a nicer person to be around.

When I dance with someone at the milonga, I do it to *really* dance with them, whether they are Javier Rodriguez or the rawest beginner. I give them my softest, nicest embrace, I listen in to how they are moving and, above all, I dive deep, deep, deep, *deep* into the music and let it move me. At other times and in other places, I teach a little and learn a lot. But at the milonga, I *dance*.

Keep it zipped

There are certain things you shouldn't say to your dance partner between songs (while actually dancing, complete silence is best). There are some men I dance with who have never got through a whole *tanda* without saying something like "It's a back *ocho* there, a back *ocho*"; "Kindly put your left arm higher, right round my neck, that's it"; "What was *that?*" (when I decorated rather enthusiastically); "Would you mind putting your head on this side" (uttered by a guy who put so much pressure on my head in the requested position that my neck ached) or "make sure you extend your leg fully in that back step, it will look prettier".

Like one rotten apple in the barrel, one impatient, irritated or grumpy remark can ruin a *tanda*. If you find yourself making such remarks often or if you think "So-and-so's dancing would be perfect if they just did X and Y, I'll make sure to remind them when we dance": *chill*. At the milonga, we dance imperfectly with imperfect partners. But you, and they, will get the most pleasure relaxed and in a state of flow.

Don't destroy that by being Mr Grumpypants.

More things not to say mid-tanda

Don't say "I think I am boring you" or any version of "you clearly don't like dancing with me." (What your partner may hear is "your dance is lacklustre and uninspiring").

Don't go on at great length about the amazing *tanda* you just danced with someone else.

Don't complain about how small your follower/leader is (do you expect them to grow taller on demand?) or how tall he/she is (you are not Procrustes).

Personally, I also have a slight preference not to receive effusive compliments until the end of the *tanda* (if someone says to me, after the first song, "wow, you are an amazing dancer," I sometimes feel a twinge of performance anxiety at wanting to live up to their first impressions – consider waiting for the *cortina* for the compliments we all love to receive).

And, if you are not sure whether or not your partner enjoyed the dance, please don't say, "we will dance another *tanda* later, definitely, I promise" (which will fill them with dread). Or, even worse, threaten, "I will come and get you for the Caló *tanda*. Make sure you save it for me."

And definitely don't ask, "well, what do you think of my dancing?"

Don't complain about lack of 'connection'

My friend: I was *really* enjoying my dances with him for the first two songs. And then he suddenly said "I feel there is a lack of connection between us. You're not really willing to connect with me. You're not giving yourself to me fully."

When you're dancing tango, you may feel close to the person because of your physical proximity, but you don't actually have access to their minds.

You know how you hate it when people second guess what you are thinking and feeling? And how they can astound and frustrate you with the degree to which they get it wrong? Let's all bear this in mind when dancing and leave the pop psychology and mind-reading games out of the embrace.

On the importance of deodorant

Mr Foreign Man (or Woman), I understand that back home you aren't considered smelly. That very faint hint of musty Camembert your armpits emit reminds you of a pleasing vintage cheese. After all, tango is about intimate physical contact, right? You count as a good dancer back home; women (or men) are used to putting up with a few sour armpit smells now and again. That might be fine in Europe, where I've rarely danced at a milonga without catching at least a few whiffs of body odour.

But it's really *not* OK here in Buenos Aires. The women here (including foreign residents like myself) have very sensitive noses because we are used to guys who don't smell *even faintly* of BO. The only fragrances to meet our nostrils are soap powder and cologne.

Plus, I am afraid of getting scent-marked by you and causing wrinkled nostrils myself. So wash under your armpits (don't just splash them with water: use soap and lather up). Use your strongest deodorant liberally. And change into a clean shirt. Repeat these three steps several times a day, even, no *especially*, if you believe that you don't need to, that you personally don't smell.

The three tanda rule

I often hear that a woman should never dance more than three *tandas* per night with the same man. I'm told that this will make him believe you are looking for sex, will put other men off dancing with you and will mark you out as a shameless hussy. Here in Buenos Aires, it is uncommon to dance more than two (non-consecutive) *tandas* with the same partner per evening, but that is simply because there is a wider choice of partners here and we hardened creatures of the *porteño* night have many opportunities to embrace. But I have danced multiple (non-consecutive) *tandas* with the same men on many occasions – and at *La Viruta Práctica* and *El Motivo*, where they don't play *tandas*, I've frequently spent most of the night in a single pair of encircling arms. Far from having to wear a giant blood-red letter A on my tango dresses or noticing people whispering and tutting as I pass, so far no one has ever batted a smokily made-up eyelid.

This urban legend is particularly pernicious to beginner women. If you go to a big grown-up milonga when you are still a tango toddler, you may well find it intimidating. You may notice a lot of eyes slide past you in the search for more desirable partners, or find yourself looking sheepishly down at the floor a lot: because you are having an off night; you shouldn't have drunk that second glass of champers; those D'Arienzos are scarily fast; or you're not sure if you can keep up with the men's furious *giros*. But, if you are a musical dancer with a soft embrace, there may be one man – maybe two – who wants to take you under his wing. Because, despite your wobbly steps, uncertainty and lack of technique, the two of you are well suited, physically, biomechanically and musically. Or maybe you will find someone with whom you have a little bit of sexual chemistry – which can go a LONG way when skill is lacking.

That's why beginner dancers are especially prone to dancing repeat *tandas* – especially sensitive beginners.

And that's totally fine. What's the worst that can happen? A guy might hit on you? If you are afraid of that, don't come to Argentina!

Multiple tandas

At a normal milonga, I much prefer it when people dance only one *tanda* at a time. It's a custom which has a tendency to optimise, though it cannot guarantee, people's tango happiness.

However, a local milonga is a very different occasion from a festival or marathon. At those events, people discover or are reunited with favourite dance partners. This may be their only chance to enjoy the blissful experience of dancing with those individuals in months, perhaps years. No wonder they want to dance multiple *tandas* – even when the connection between them is not sexual or romantic but "only" blissful dance floor compatibility, a beautiful and precious thing.

At those special events, both partners tend to hover around near each other during the *cortinas*. If I enjoy the guy's dancing, I wait for his cues. He might hug me and say "thank you," ending our stint of dances – or ask "shall we see what the DJ plays next?" In the latter case, I'll say "sure." If the chemistry between us is very intense, there usually comes a point at which he no longer asks, but we just stand in silence between *tandas*, not daring to break the spell.

As for the idea that, if multiple *tandas* were not permitted, leaders would dance with a wider range of women, I'm sceptical. Most good dancers are very selective about who they dance with. Partners are not interchangeable for them. If you stop me from dancing with people I enjoy, that *won't* make me dance with people I *don't* enjoy dancing with. I'll take no dances over bad or mediocre dances any time.

The ideal situation is to be part of a tango scene in which suitable and willing partners abound at every milonga, you see your favourite partners at least once a week and the milonga is seven hours long and stuffed with your favourite boys. But we don't all dance in ideal situations. I prefer a culture in which people dance one *tanda* at a time. But I don't regret a single one of the occasions on which I danced multiple consecutive *tandas*. They were thrilling experiences, every one. As I danced with one special man last night, I was keenly aware of the very real possibility that I might never be able to dance with him again. And it made me not want to leave his arms.

Sometimes it's better to break tanda

Last night, I noticed a friend break *tanda* after one song. It was quick, surgically precise and, at that informal milonga, fairly discreet. There was no way of telling who initiated the separation, him or her, or for what reason. I am very reluctant to break *tanda*, but it's a useful tool. We should not frivolously abandon people mid-*tanda* for no good reason. But sometimes but you simply *cannot* make it work. It might not be anyone's fault. Continuing to dance with the partner may not even help save face, since observers may notice the strain in your expression, the misery in your eyes or the little line forming between your brows.

If you take chances on random partners sight unseen, you need an emergency brake. Be patient if the partner is clearly a beginner. But if they are someone with ingrained habits which – whether due to your own shortcomings or theirs – you find so overwhelmingly irritating that the *tanda* becomes agony, put them out of their misery. Just take a deep breath and say "thank you."

Sometimes I feel "God, I would love to break *tanda* now, but I'll grit my teeth and get through it. I don't want to make the guy feel bad." Under those circumstances, I try my best to disguise what I'm feeling. The occasional bad dance is an inevitable side effect of the fact that I sometimes take chances on a *cabeceo* from a complete stranger.

But when that happens, nine times out of ten, I find the partner breaks *tanda* with me. Just as I am mentally berating him for being an insensitive oaf who is throwing me around as if I were a marionette, he proves to me that he *does* have a clear perception of what I am feeling and of how well or otherwise our dance is working. Just as I am counting down the seconds to the *cortina*, my partner releases me from my obligations with a merciful "thank you." This strengthens my faith in humanity since it shows that people are often more sensitive than we give them credit for.

Mutually-desired dances are the best. For *both* parties. Many people are sensitive enough to tell when their partner is not enjoying the dance. And that eliminates their own pleasure in it.

Hey, it's OK

I read women's magazines, which often have a section at the back, giving readers permission to do certain things (read everything written on your crush's Facebook wall since 2009; spend the whole day in pyjamas binge-watching *The Great British Bake Off*; prefer *In Style Magazine* to Dostoevsky, etc.). The section is usually called *Hey, it's OK...* Here's my tango version:

Hey, it's OK...

to hate a particular orchestra but still leap up to dance to it if you get a chance to dance with someone *really* special just when that orchestra comes on

to break the *tanda* just because of someone's BO. (*ew!* don't get that smell on me!)

to not recognise the orchestra or blank on it when asked (even if it's Pugliese, D'Arienzo or Di Sarli)

to feel like just sitting morosely drinking beer and watching

to dance with someone just because they are so gorgeous you want to rub up against them in close embrace

to camp it up and make your movements big and dramatic on an almost-empty floor

to backlead occasionally (sometimes you have to make an executive decision) to feel a little peeved when your gorgeous visiting best friend dances all night with all the partners you've been eyeing longingly, without success, for literally years (it's probably best to sit separately, though, if you find you get eaten up with envy)

to practise your most seductive *mirada* on random good-looking strangers in ordinary life

to wear lower-heeled shoes if the very high ones hurt your feet, challenge your balance or turn you into a giant – or for any reason you like

to wear very high-heeled tango shoes to a women's technique class (it's good training for your balance), even though you are in possession of a Y chromosome and had to special order the shoes in size 47

to get mesmerised by the sight of yourself in a mirror or by a video of your dancing because of how great you look (the Greeks were onto something with that Narcissus story)

to do leg caress or foot capture decorations just because it feels fun to play footsie

to fake injury to escape from a truly disastrous *tanda* – and to make a miraculous recovery in time for the start of the next *tanda* (ice, rubbing it and making pouty faces can have remarkable curative effects)

to be really happy you dance tango because it gives you lots of opportunities to wear that sharp suit/silk dress/pair of shiny red stilettos

to want to dance every single *tanda*

Milonga Culture in Buenos Aires and Beyond

—What's a "milonga"?
—Basically, it's a room full of people walking around in a circle.

* * *

You know you're in Buenos Aires when...
they play The Gotan Project as a *cortina*, secure in the knowledge that no one will dance to it
you can wear a tight skirt to the milonga, secure in the knowledge that no one will *gancho* you.

* * *

"I was expecting a much more formal atmosphere, with people who weren't dancing listening to the music in reverential silence. The fact that men and women sit separately made me think it would be a bit like the Russian Orthodox Church I grew up with. Or like a synagogue. But it's not at all solemn. It's a party." (*The Jackrabbit* on *Cachirulo*)

* * *

The dancers make the milonga

What makes a milonga for me? Good dancers who will dance with me. The music comes a close second – but partly because if the dancers don't like the music they won't dance much. It's also lovely to have a great sound system, a beautiful floor, wine, food, an attractive venue and friendly people.

My idea of 'good dancers' may be different from yours. Tastes differ. But it's the *dancers* who make my evening.

I've had a lot of wonderful nights in Buenos Aires at grungy venues with rock-hard floors, where the music sounded as though it were coming from underwater, where I embraced soaking-wet men and in tropical temperatures, where visiting the toilets was a venture requiring enormous fortitude and the coffee tasted like diesel fuel. But having a really good partner in your arms can turn the gloomiest, most cockroach-infested fleapit into twelve minutes of paradise.

Milonga Culture in Baires

Milonga ecosystems

The milonga is an undefined public space where lots of social groups coexist, sometimes interacting and sometimes not. At times, it feels like a pub. If you go to a bar or pub on your own, you don't expect everyone there to chat to you or even pay you any attention. They might, but if they do it's a bonus.

And sometimes being at the milonga feels like being part of a club, or being at your local boozer where you recognise all the old familiar faces, the local mix of friends, acquaintances, neighbours, relatives, rivals and enemies (often overlapping categories). And sometimes it feels like a dinner party, where almost everyone is a close friend-of-a-friend.

The more often you attend the same milonga, the more it approaches the feel of a dinner party and the further it seems from the anonymity of a bar. But it's a social phenomenon and, as such, is diverse, organic and constantly evolving. Some people only like dancing with their friends – that's fine. Some only like dancing with the really good dancers (and are lucky enough to be desirable partners for them too) – that's also fine. They all pay their entrance fees and help to keep the milonga financially afloat. They all add to the vibe.

Tango here in Buenos Aires isn't a landscaped park; it's a forest. A lot of the resentments that fester in diaspora communities stem from people trying to impose their own narrow definitions on the milonga and make everyone behave in accordance with their own vision. But planned economies never work. You won't be able to create a benevolent dictatorship. You have to work with people's differing desires when it comes to choosing their dance partners, their social interactions, their friends, their sexual partners and (within reason) their behaviour at the milonga.

Generalisations you can and can't make about Baires milongas

In Buenos Aires, our tango scene encompasses a wide range of *prácticas* and milongas: the trendy young *salony* scenes full of the youthful, lithe and beautiful; the pot-haze-clouded grungy bohemian places where payment is collected by passing a hat; the traditional dancers at *El Maipú*; the men at *Lo de Celia* who are still playful and unruly during the fast Canaro milongas after sixty years on the dance floors of the city; the pretty gay boys at *La Marshàll*; the mob scene at *Canning* where the composition of dancers shifts over the course of the evening, from many tourists and beginners elbowing each other on the crowded *pista* to the lovely dance fireworks of the late-night almost-empty floor; the older men circling the room to do their walking *cabeceos* under the pink neon sign of *Gricel*; the intimate close-embrace-only nights at tiny *La Piccola*; the young professional couples letting off steam in thrilling displays of virtuosic, joyful musicality at *El Yeite*; the men in suits and slicked-back hair and the women in sparkly dresses and careful make-up at *Sunderland*.

The scene here is big: it's multi-faceted, fickle and subject to trends (though some milongas seem to never change). It encompasses a wide range of social customs and ways of dancing. There are some *almost* constants here: the absence of alternative or 'non' tango music and people's fierce insistence on liberty of partner choice (if a good dancer doesn't want to dance with you, you *cannot* make them). But, as far as pretty much every other generalisation goes, all bets are off.

When you hear "in Buenos Aires they would never...," add the mental caveat "at certain milongas, that is." Buenos Aires is complex. That's part of its charm. But don't worry, the reigning customs and mores of each individual milonga quickly become obvious after a little observation. You'll work it out.

How to enjoy yourself at Baires milongas as a visitor

Any new tango scene can be difficult to break into. Buenos Aires probably more than most. This is the largest scene in the world and people have a greater choice of good partners here than anywhere else. Add to this the fact that, during high season, there is a huge influx of visitors from abroad. If you are a first-time visitor, you may find that you are not the partner everyone has been longing for all their lives, nor will there be a stampede to take you out onto the *pista*. Many people already dance as much as they want to, without needing to ever seek out anyone new.

Many people hope that here in Baires they will be able to dance with partners they wouldn't encounter at home or who, at home, would not choose to dance with them. But trying to get dances with people who are better dancers than you is always tricky (though, with patience, luck and good humour, it's often possible). Pressurising, bullying, blackmailing, chatting up or guilt-tripping people will absolutely *not* work here. Most people here will not dance with you just because you're friends or to be polite. This is a culture in which we are used to separating friendliness from an obligation to dance and where many people are fiercely protective of their right to free partner choice at the milonga. So much so, that many social norms have evolved to safeguard those rights, most obviously the practice of *mirada/cabeceo*.

Come to learn, observe, take classes, improve your dancing and dance for mutual enjoyment: whether with other foreign visitors or with Argentines, whether with people whose dance skills are close to your own level of proficiency or higher. Dances with the better dancers can leave you utterly blissed out and if you are patient and choose your milongas with care, you may well find that bliss here. But ditch the idea that you are somehow owed it.

People at the milongas are there for their own enjoyment. For them, that might mean sitting drinking and chatting to friends or only dancing with people they know, only with their girlfriends or boyfriends, or only with those whose dancing is at a certain level of skill or musicality. Or perhaps they only dance with people who've trained in a specific style or with women they find attractive. Some may enjoy taking chances on complete unknowns or be willing to dance with almost everyone. All those options are equally valid. And none of them are really any of your business, any more than, if you were at a bar, whether someone ordered wine, orange juice or gin and tonic.

Tango here is a pleasure, not a duty. The Argentines are a pretty open nation (perhaps partly because of their mongrel heritage and veritable tsunamis of immigrants). Many of us here in Buenos Aires look forward to the arrival of visitor dancers because we love extending our circle of dance partners. But always remember that, at the milonga, your pleasure is no more important than anyone else's. You might find that you end up having an unexpectedly wonderful time. But there are no guarantees.

What's expected from you here in Baires

Being back in Buenos Aires is like going from a stroll in a manicured city park to a bracing hike on the moors. You have to up your game, put that Ferrari into fifth gear and whip yourself into shape.

No one is going to dance with you out of friendship or obligation – you've got to give them a *reason* to dance with you and that reason is usually that you would be lovely to dance with.

If you're a leader, you need to manage that whirling, fast-paced, slightly hectic floor. Many people count on other advanced dancers' fast reactions and sophisticated musicality to avoid collisions (and it usually works).

Then there is the dynamic quality of the dancing. It's fast paced (except in huge dramatic suspended pauses); it's twisty, with a thousand changes of direction, strewn with syncopations and bursts of explosive speed. People are doing much more and doing it much faster than in many diaspora scenes, where I've had many extremely enjoyable dances, but rarely felt pushed to my limits as a dancer.

Then there is what they are expecting of you as a follower. You not only *can* decorate – you'd bloody well *better* decorate with musicality and precision. It's not only that you are *able* to really actively dance your steps, but that you are *expected* to embody the music. The dance is a dialogue and you are not just gallantly permitted to have your say; you're expected to have something interesting to tell. When you are led an *ocho*, say, you have to dance it in the exact timing that you are hearing in the music at that moment – and the leaders are lightning quick at adjusting to whatever you do. Plus, the leaders are listening polyphonically, hearing the deeper layers of the music as well as the most obvious surface sounds and are therefore prepared for the followers to play with more subtle musical elements.

The younger leaders are looking for followers with character, confidence and chutzpah, full partners in the game. You can't just follow – you'd better *dance*, bitches.

It's strong dancing. You can't be timid or apologetic. You need fast reaction times, you need to turn on a dime and pounce on detail in the music. And, it doesn't matter if you are the best dancer back home – you won't be the best here. Because people like Cecilia and Serkan, Adriana and Fernando, Noelia and Carlitos, Gaston and Moira are out there on the floor, setting the pace. You'll need to give it your all to try to keep up.

I'm always glad to be back.

Why I don't call them tango tourists

I'm not a fan of the word "tourist" to describe people visiting Buenos Aires to dance tango. The word has connotations of frivolity, superficiality and more cash than sense: "tourist" has a quite different valence from "traveller," "explorer," etc. And, while there is nothing wrong with being a tourist in *any* sense of the word, the superficial implications are inappropriate in this context.

These people haven't come to Buenos Aires because it's an exotic-sounding Latin American city. They've come because they have a connection with this place, through their love of its urban folk dance. They aren't touring; they are immersing themselves, however briefly, in the local tango culture. They are learning to connect the dance with its geographical origins, its homeland.

And when I hear "who wants to dance with tourists?" "ugh, this place is full of tourists!"; "there are too many tourists here"; "I danced with x, but it didn't count because he is a tourist" (things I hear mostly from other foreigners), it makes me very sad. Argentines and foreigners, tourists and locals: those are irrelevant categories. You don't embrace a nation; you embrace an individual. Many of my tanguero friends abroad are supporting Argentina in the World Cup – because when you dance tango you feel a little Argentine, even if you have never set foot in this hemisphere.

Tango is a country of which we are all citizens. That's why I don't talk about "tourists." I call them visiting dancers. If that's you – welcome!

Low versus high season in Buenos Aires

It happens as suddenly as flicking a switch: the turn from an Indian summer to a crisp, bright-skied autumn. Suddenly everyone disappears and off-season is upon us.

Buenos Aires often feels like a seaside resort: bustling in the warmer months of our long summer, when we pack into *Canning* like sweaty sardines, almost dying of thirst as we wait seemingly hours for the harried waitress to make her rounds; when there are no seats at *Milonga 10* and I am always trapped hovering by the toilets and the floor is a whirling bumper car ride with the tables around the edge bouncing with the impact of high *boleos* (leaders usually direct *boleos* outwards, for obvious reasons, and the furniture suffers); when it is pointless to get to *Cachirulo* after 10pm or you will be squeezed into a back row seat from whence *cabeceo* is impossible without a terrestrial telescope.

I love the buzz and excitement of high season, the seemingly endless supply of good dancers, the thrill of dancing *tanda* after *tanda*; floors still crowded at 5am and famous dancers giving masterclasses; the excitement of trying to get *cabeceos* from unknown Korean and Japanese boys who you have just seen circling the *ronda* with beautiful elegance.

Now, things have died back down. Our seaside town is officially off season and we are taking the deckchairs indoors and closing the ice cream stand. There are advantages. Rooms are cheaper; there is more individual attention at classes; milongas are lower-key – and there are chances to dance with those who were too busy with other partners during the frenetic days of summer. We are mostly among ourselves now, we residents of this crazy city.

But Buenos Aires in low season is still better than high season anywhere else I've ever danced.

Venturing out into the unknown

The tango lifestyle is an odd one in many ways. Sometimes I pick a milonga I've never been to before, and head off on a long bus journey to a *barrio* I don't know well. In some respects, we have no idea what is going to happen, whether it will be a wonderful night or a deathly boring one, whether we will be The Dancing Queen or a neglected wallflower. But, in other ways, we know exactly what to expect. Whilst I would never cross this city to go to an unknown bar or club in a potentially dodgy neighbourhood and stay out till the wee small hours, at the milonga, I know exactly what to expect. I can already picture the tiled floor, the tables around the edge, the glasses brimming with Malbec, the older guys in suits and the women in handkerchief-hemmed polyester. And – to a lesser extent – we can have similar experiences all over the world.

Milongas which are focused on socialising

There are a variety of different milongas here in Buenos Aires: at some, most people are there primarily to dance. As the *tanda* begins, many pairs of eyes start scrutinising the room avidly, hoping to give or catch a *cabeceo*. Those not dancing are mostly watching the floor, observing the dancers. A few of them might be chatting in a casual manner, with at least half their attention still on the main attraction, the floor (which is like a giant television set in its ability to captivate people and prevent serious conversation).

Then there are those milongas where many people are standing around, chatting to friends, drinking a sweating bottle of Quilmes or three. Where some people come without even bringing their tango shoes. Where even the Di Sarli-Rufino *tanda* doesn't distract people from intense conversations, flirtations and large slices of pizza. They might dance a few *tandas* – or not.

I'm happy that both kinds of milongas exist. I like to feel I am among friends at the milonga and to chat during the occasional *tanda* if I'm not dancing. But I've never been very good at milonga-time socialising. Always, at least half my focus is on the music, the dancers and my own wish to dance.

Even after so many years here in Buenos Aires, play me a Laurenz *tanda* and my mind and body will instantly, automatically gear up for dancing. My heart will be beating slightly faster, my bottom wiggling the tiniest bit on my seat, my eyes scanning the room for potential partners.

That's why formal milongas are my favourites. I love it when everyone is there with one sole purpose: tango bliss. Because, although I enjoy chatting to friends over a glass of wine, what I *really* love is to dance.

Long live traditional milongas

The formal milonga is a unique social space. Most people arrive on their own – in fact, I recommend flying solo, for maximum chances of great dances. You won't feel like a social reject if you don't know a soul. You won't need to schmooze, chat or hang around hoping for a dance or wish you were part of the 'cool' crowd. It's neither an outing with friends, nor an evening of solitude. Good dancers everywhere tend to be coy with their favours at first. But most of my visitor friends have found it easier to get dances at the formal milongas and have found their social politics less complex and confusing. The codes (the *tandas* and *cortinas*, the split seating, the practice of *mirada/cabeceo*) are less like the forms of normal social interaction, but they are also more clear cut, unambiguous and transparent and easier to master. You just have to dress well, follow the rules, and dance to the best of your ability, not try to decipher a myriad subtle signals and negotiate strata upon strata of sociological groupings.

As a woman, you can feel totally comfortable and secure expressing clearly that you want to dance with *that man there*. There's no pretence, no game-playing. If you want to dance with someone, you look right at them, clear in the eyes.

It's a space where you can have warm, tender, sweet, intimate contact and communication with the opposite sex. Where you hold attractive people in your arms without fear of encountering a creep or coming over as one, without having to be cautious or defensive, needing drugs to get you high or fearing sexual harassment or assault. Without needing anyone's protection, without feeling desperate or pushy.

It's a space where, as a single person, you may feel frustrated if you are not getting dances, but you won't feel friendless, lonely, like a social outcast, rejected or sad. It's not like being alone at a restaurant, bar or cinema among groups of laughing friends and hand-holding lovers. You're totally independent – and yet in the best company, among your fellow-dancers, where you need feel no shame. You're not going to get drunk, take E, damage your eardrums and snog someone that you will regret the next morning. You're there to dedicate yourself to a beautiful art form. You're there for the best of reasons. To dance.

The formal milonga is a unique social experience. It's a place which can unite us all in twelve-minute hugs: old and young of every nationality, colour and creed. It's the opposite of a swingers club: a place not of casual sex, but of casual love.

Let's hear it for the traditional milonga. Because, right now, this is the kind of space we humans need.

Simple instructions on how to work it at a formal, split-seating milonga in Buenos Aires. For the new and bewildered.

1. Before you arrive, shower and choose your clothing carefully, especially men. If you look the part, it will be much easier for you to get those initial *tandas* as an unknown. I recommend a freshly-laundered, ironed, long-sleeved shirt and slacks for guys. A jacket is a nice touch. Shave meticulously and wear your strongest deodorant and a subtle dab of cologne. Women: wear whatever you like, as long as it's not grungy. Men: no jeans or dance sneakers. Women: no flat shoes. Wear kitten heels if you're not comfortable in high stilettos.

2. Call to book and show up nice and early. It really is worth it to get a good seat. Your sightlines are going to be crucial.

3. Wait for the organiser to seat you. If you only want to dance with the friends you came with or with your girlfriend/boyfriend, ask to be seated together. Otherwise, tell the organiser that you are on your own or with same sex friends only and let them seat you in the section appropriate to your personal chromosomal configuration. If you are seated very far back or shoved away into a corner, it can be worth *very politely* asking if there are any better seats available. But don't whinge or make a scene or the organiser will probably seat you right in front of the toilets. Bear in mind that sightlines will improve later in the evening and it may even be possible to change seats when some of the early birds leave (always ask first). Men also have the

36

option of hanging out at the bar – women do too, though that's less common. That can give you a different view and therefore new potential partners.

4. Make friends with your seat neighbours. They'll be able to alert you to a desirable partner who is looking unnoticed in your direction, recommend good dancers and warn you of who to avoid. Flag down the waiter as soon as you can and order water and/or wine.

5. Get those peepers ready. It's *cabeceo* time. Remember: wait till the beginning of the *tanda*, be clear, be decisive, be speedy. Women, stay seated till the guy is standing right in front of you and you are certain the *cabeceo* was aimed at you.

6. Men: for extra brownie points, walk the women back to their seats at the end of the *tanda*. Congratulations! You have now been baptised and are an official devotee of the tango gods at this particular shrine.

A few things to avoid:

Don't walk up to people and ask them to dance. You risk not only a brusque rejection, but invoking the wrath of the organiser. Women, don't accept verbal invitations from lurkers. When you entered the formal milonga, you made a tacit agreement to handle all requests the ocular way. (Unless you're sitting at a table with friends or a partner or under exceptional circumstances.)

Don't get up to dance with someone of your own sex. This might be OK at SOME milongas, under SOME circumstances (for milonga or during the final *tanda* of the night). But if in doubt, don't, unless you are a rebel who doesn't mind making a statement at the risk of being asked to leave.

Don't throw a hissy fit at the way things are handled at a formal milonga. There are a dozen other milongas you could be at instead. If you prefer a different atmosphere, you have choices.

Don't be scared. If you get a few things 'wrong,' you will not be placed in the stocks. It's actually pretty relaxed. People are there to party, after all! This is their fun night out.

Personally, I love the formal milongas because of their mixed age, mixed level and strong focus on dancing, rather than socialising. They are my favourite places to dance.

Cliquey milongas

There are two approaches to the milonga: you can turn up on your own and find dances with whoever happens to be there. Or you can book a table and show up with a group of friends. While I generally prefer to go stag, the second option has a lot of advantages, especially if your group is roughly gender balanced and you all enjoy dancing with each other.

Some milongas are quite difficult places to get dances if you arrive alone. Some, like *Sunderland* and *La Baldosa*, are known for being couple and group heavy, most dancers focus their attention on their own table and cross-room *cabeceos* are relatively rare.

At some places, such as *Canning* in high season, the sheer size of the room, coupled with the crowding, makes long-range *mirada/cabeceo* almost impossible during peak hours, while most people will (not always politely) refuse invitations offered verbally at their table. *Cabeceo* cruising is a good potential solution to this, but many people (including me) feel uncomfortably stalker-ish when they practise it.

Then there is *El Yeite*, where the *pista* is often a spectacular display of beautiful dancing by young professionals of galactic level. If you want to dance much, you'd be well advised to come accompanied by your own group of fellow earthlings.

In all those situations, it's reassuring to know that you will have at least a few good *tandas* with your opposite-role friends. It's comforting to know that, if the milonga is not too formal, you can change into your flat shoes and lead your female friends. It's practical to share a taxi and a bottle of wine, a table.

So, many of us go to the milonga, at least some of the time, in a group. From within my group table, I am always craning my head around, trying to catch dances. New discoveries fill me with glee and I am tempted to high five my friends and notch the heel of my stiletto when I've captured a new twelve-minute victim.

But people who have never danced with me before are difficult birds to flush out of hiding, so it's nice to have a few feathered creatures in the hand. So that, my friends, is why some milongas can be cliquey. But remember that a clique is just a group of friends you aren't part of. Yet.

Cachirulo and the milongas at El Beso

The floor at El Beso

A familiar smell can evoke many memories. The powdery floral aroma of *Anaïs Anaïs* conjures up an image of my mother in the late 70s, squeezing the bulb of an old perfume bottle and arching her neck towards the spray.

The feel of the *El Beso* floor underfoot sets off as powerful a chain of associations as any scent. For us dancers, the relationship with the floor is primary. It's more than just the surface beneath our shoes. It's our ally, our partner, our shelter. Stepping out onto it feels like an immersion, like diving into a buoyant pool, like Cleopatra dipping her limbs into her bath of asses' milk. It's a different world, a world where movements have a gliding effortlessness.

The pale sprung wooden floor of *El Beso* is the dream floor, like a concert hall with optimum acoustics to an opera singer, like the perfect play of soft evening light to a photographer. As the soles of my shoes make contact, it feels like wrapping my lips around the first heaped teaspoonful of the creamiest, richest chocolate mousse, like burying my nose in the most decadent rose at the height of its bloom, like enveloping my freshly-moisturised body in a silk robe. It's my somatic madeleine: my feet remember this sensation. If you can dance well elsewhere, you will be in heaven here.

The golden hour at El Beso

There is nothing like the last hour of *El Beso*, when the smooth pool of the floor is only sparsely populated with dancers, when there is room to lap up the *pista* in big strides and whirl through *giros*. The freedom of movement feels all the sweeter after an evening nestled amid other couples in cosy proximity, like a long hike in the Scottish Highlands after a frantic workweek in London.

There are few things as exhilarating as that feeling of space. At rush hour last night, around 1am, I danced a D'Arienzo *tanda* in which I scarcely moved from the spot. We stood there hugging each other for three minutes at a time. And then, only two hours later, *El Beso* had metamorphosed. My legs flew in their highest *boleos* and I lifted my free foot in big arcs, cutting curves through the air, painting hoops and circles for the sheer joy of claiming my airspace. We circled each other in huge *giros* and I bent my standing knee deep to let my foot trace the largest *planeo* it could as it swept round to axis in *parada*.

I love to dance in crowded spaces, with teeny tiny steps. But I really love the relief when the evening grows late, the DJ busts out the dramatic music and there is room to splash and play. If you always dance in places with plenty of room, you'll never know quite the same thrill.

Sundays at El Beso

No milonga makes me feel quite as much at home as *El Beso* on a Sunday night. I feel like a regular at the cosiest of local pubs, a Japanese man when they pour *sake* for him from his own bottle, kept behind the bar. I have my seat (in a prime position); I know and love Lucía Plazaola's music selections; I recognise the regulars and can reliably divide those among them whose dancing I admire into two groups: those with whom I almost always dance a *tanda* or two and those who have never given me a *cabeceo* and perhaps never will – though I still cast a few hopeful *miradas* in their direction from time to time. Everything is reassuringly familiar: Susanna, the organiser; the handsome waiters; the glasses of Chandon; the short-sighted guy who needs a *mirada* strong enough for Lasik surgery; the acerbic humour of the older woman in lacy leggings; the *Son of a Preacher Man cortina*; the gossip and laughter with my table neighbours; the 'reviews' of visiting dancers ("*Oooh,* have you danced with that tall, lanky Asian chap, is he any good? Is that black guy nice to dance with?"); the chubby older guys who hold me in comfortingly firm but unconstricting hearty, huggy embraces and the cute young boys who embrace with a lovely softness.

I dance almost every *tanda*: from the funked-up Biagis to the bubbly Fresedos, from the dense Puglieses to the hysterical D'Arienzos. I have one *tanda* of agony (my neighbours commiserate) and the rest of the time I feel snugly immersed in the music, a baroque miniaturist in my decorations.

I take second helpings of the most delicious dancers. I lament the lack of a De Angelis *tanda* because I really need a break to eat a toasted sandwich – *ah*, perhaps now; *oh no!* not now, it's Laurenz! and *not now*, it's Di Sarli with Rufino, it's Donato milongas, it's Troilo with Marino... *Aaaaaah!*

To me, this is the ideal milonga, this is what I think of when you say the word 'milonga'. This is my local place, this is my tango home.

When waiters turn dancers

"My old man was quite the tanguero in his day. I grew up listening to the music at home. I've always loved the music. But I never believed *I* could dance: look at me. I've got two left feet. But then, while working here, seeing everyone embracing each other, dancing, it's so beautiful. So now I'm taking lessons." [Waiter at *El Beso*.]

All the waiters at my favourite milonga now dance tango – and began learning after watching us punters swirl around the floor in close embrace. It warms my heart. We should keep organising the flash mobs, dancing in the front rooms of venues with shop windows facing the street, in the street markets, in the parks, in the open air and in the public spaces. Because, even danced clumsily or awkwardly, tango is beautiful. Forget the pigeon-toed feet and the jutting hips: just look up, to head level. Look at the arms wrapped around each other. Look at the faces of concentration and bliss. It's a sight which makes you feel: right there, in those arms, *that's* where I want to be.

The microcosm that is Cachirulo

Sometimes, I don't need pretty *lápices* and big walking turns. Sometimes, I just want to grab the guy, envelop him in a giant two-tit embrace and really feel his body as we dance. Sometimes it's nice to dance in sustained close embrace all night. That's why I love *Cachirulo*.

At *Cachirulo* last night, as I danced my way through almost all my familiar partners and made a few additional discoveries, I felt as though the intervening week had been a dream and I had woken back up to reality again. The space is so familiar to me – my beloved *El Beso* – so many of the faces are well-known and the embraces well-loved and the milonga is so long (the six hours passed with incredible speed), that it felt almost like going to the office, in some topsy-turvy world dedicated to pleasure, not work.

No matter what the weather is like outside, inside there is always a slight chill, just enough to require a cardigan over your shoulders if you sit out a *tanda*. Always, Hector places me in a corner seat, from which *mirada* is a challenge, but I take pride in being able to use my ocular sniper skills to great effect, even over longer distances. Always, I greet the waiters with a kiss and order my aeroplane-sized bottle of sour Argentine champers.

Always, there are minor miracles. The favourite partner sitting at the diametrically opposite corner with the light behind him so I couldn't see his eyes who was sneakily able to ask me to dance verbally when he returned a dance partner to her seat next to mine as the *cortina* ended. "Want to dance?" he whispered discreetly and I leaped up with delight. The young guy I had never seen before who caught my eye from afar, who invited me with a single confident nod and took me on a smooth, floaty trip around the floor in multiple open embrace *giros*, with all the unmistakable hallmarks of a Carlitos Pérez student. The old favourite partners with whom I can play more, who understand me better every time, who smile and laugh and hug me, with whom I have a relationship that is developing week by week, month by month, year by year, growing ever subtler and richer.

We can catch a stranger's eye and seconds later be in his arms and feel as though we had danced with each other for years. We can adapt and adjust to many partners, of a wide range of ages and nationalities, each with their own idiosyncratic ways of hearing the music and holding the other person and with each of them it can feel so natural, easy and free, that I don't feel as though I were following the leader at all, but just expressing the music spontaneously, following the impulses of my own body, not knowing if they originated in something he led or in something I heard on the violin at that moment – making the togetherness, the harmonious joint movement, the transformation into "a beautiful four-legged monster" (as Peter Litser puts it) all the more miraculous.

I treasure the little bubble of happiness, the special space, curtained off from the sadness, poverty and violence of the wider world, the place of bliss which is my favourite milonga.

Dancing with another woman at El Beso

The only thing I dislike about formal milongas is the embargo on dancing with people of your own sex. No one has ever been able to give me a convincing argument why not – although many people have told me that it just "isn't right," it "doesn't represent tango" or "gives them a bad feeling": arguments which remind me of those who think homosexuality should not be legal "because it's icky."

If we accept that two men or two women can fall in love, have sex, get married and adopt children, there is no reason why we cannot accept that they should dance tango with each other.

I'm not a rebel. But I still remember the first time I got up and danced with another woman at *El Beso*. I broke the rules just a tiny bit, choosing milonga, rather than tango – which is taken less seriously and in which I therefore felt less exposed. I kept my eyes open and, over my friend's shoulder, I saw a lot of wide-eyed, startled faces and one or two frowning looks. A Japanese friend was giggling nervously. But the world did not end. My friend and I were not politely asked to leave. We stayed until the end, dancing every *tanda* (with men). We were warmly hugged good night by the organiser. "Did you enjoy yourself tonight?" I asked her later. "Oh yes," she said, "but my favourite part was breaking the rules."

Breaking the rules at Cachirulo – and getting away with it.

I have a confession to make. All night long, I'd been catching tantalising glimpses of this playful, musical leader I had never seen before, but whenever he went back to his seat, at the very opposite end of the long, bare space of *El Obelisco*, he was instantly obscured from my line of sight.

It took a long time to even see where he was seated: in the second row, behind two tall men who both started nodding and gesturing in *cabeceo* whenever I looked in his direction. Several times he craned his head towards me, cocked it at me, I nodded vigorously and then one of the tall men would start up from his chair and I would shake my head "sorry, no, not you" at which point *my* dancer would sink back in disappointment too.

At last we achieved a successful *cabeceo*, after half a dozen attempts, and went on a wonderfully fun ride through D'Arienzo together. As the last track began, he asked "Can we dance the next *tanda*, too? I have been wanting to dance with you all night." Why not? I thought. During the *cortina*, he accompanied me to my seat and, then, squeezing round the tightly-packed chairs with some difficulty, hovered behind the women's section awkwardly. As the opening bars of a Di Sarli *tanda* started, I turned round and received a very close-range *cabeceo* from him.

I like the *códigos*. But I *love* great dancing. The rules are made to serve the dancers, not vice versa. I'm sure the tango gods will pardon us.

Two eternal optimists at Cachirulo

Cachirulo will probably always be one of my favourite milongas, for lots of reasons. First of all, as a friend of mine puts it, "there's less bullshit" than at many other places. You can find it difficult to get dances there if you are a newcomer. It can be tricky to get *cabeceos* if you are unlucky enough to have a poor seat and Hector's seating arrangements can seem quite arbitrary at times; he does have a system, but it is complicated enough to be a fitting subject for a novel by Dan Brown.

But watch the floor at *Cachi* and you will see beautiful young women dancing with round-bellied older men in suits; sexy young men smilingly inviting women to dance who are old enough to be their mothers or grandmothers; rose-cheeked, velvet-skinned lovely girls ironing their buttocks while wrinkled matrons in sausage-casing tight mini-skirts are enjoying *tanda* after *tanda*. It's all about the dancing there. That's what people have come for.

And, if anyone reading is a matchmaker, there is a couple who are surely fated to be together. There is the man who walked along the entire row of women, obstructing the *ronda* while people were dancing a waltz, and, stopping solemnly in front of each table, nodded at the seated women there, in a very short-range *cabeceo*. (He didn't get a dance, but did receive many puzzled looks, raised eyebrows and disapproving mutters). His soul mate, surely, was the woman who teetered along the same row, visibly tipsy, champagne glass in hand, looking for a free seat, insisting that many chairs in succession weren't taken, since they looked empty at that moment, as their owners were dancing. Those two eternal optimists need to find each other.

Cachiruliando

It took a long time to finally get to dance with someone I had been eyeing longingly: one of the oldest men I've danced with – and one of the best. The familiar Troilo instrumentals were fresh and exciting in his arms. Even the eponymous *Cachirulo*, whose jaunty rhythms I must have heard a thousand times, gleamed as though someone had polished the dust off. He put pauses in unexpected but musically fitting places; slowed down to dance lazy legatos in time with discreet countermelodies on the violins, caught buzzy, barely-audible syncopations in the double bass; let his dance switch between instrumental lines, between song and countersong, shuffling the layers of the Troilean deck of cards. It felt like flying up and down a tower between the levels of a shell world. Beneath the worn patina of the familiar surface was a choppier, more richly diverse Troilo, notes hanging like stalactites, inviting a joint musical exploration.

And then, later, in someone else's arms, I had a different experience of depth. We had last met in an art gallery on a muggy northern summer's night, amid the flaking, fading grandeur of a central European city, the home of one of my favourite partners in the world. "We are so far from Buenos Aires," he told me then, "and yet there are people here who really care about tango." Waltzing with him I had an odd sensation, a nostalgic longing for the nostalgia of that night in Zagreb, a palimpsest of sentimentality, an emotional *mise en abîme*.[1] For once, I didn't want to decorate and play. I only wanted to feel his embrace as softly enveloping as it had been then, to use the music as my magic carpet to fly back in time. This was a Proustian embrace that revived time past, an intuitive reaction to remembered sensation.

There is more than one way to go deeper into the moment when you dance.

---

[1] In art, *mise en abîme* or *mise en abyme* is the device of placing a copy of an image within itself.

Cachi Musicality

I'm astonished, once again, by how quickly the seven hours of *Cachirulo* can pass. I was extremely tired and hungry and my plan was to stay for only an hour or two. But one and a half *empanadas* (my supper), two glasses of water, a glass of wine and two coffees later, after dancing a good two dozen *tandas* or more, I was suddenly returning to my seat after the *Cumparsita*, with sore feet, damp armpits, rumpled top, smeared eyeliner and dragged-through-a-hedge-frizzy hair. *Cachi* became satisfyingly full at peak hour, with all the many rows of chairs occupied, including the far-off seats way back from the dance floor, from which I received two deeply gratifying long-distance *cabeceos*.

The music was pleasingly different from the usual selections. I was particularly happy when, after the jaunty tones of *Cachirulo* itself ("*A bailar! CACHIRUUUUUUUUULO!*" shouted the organiser as always as he announced the milonga's eponymous track) the DJ, instead of playing Troilo instrumentals, treated us to a *tanda* of intense vocals. (I am definitely not a purist when it comes to mixing instrumental and vocal tangos.) There were also, surprisingly, several *tandas* of early and early-ish D'Arienzo instrumentals – music with which I am currently passionately in love. There was also a Varela *tanda* featuring little-known tracks of sickly sentimentality which usually languish in well-deserved obscurity. But I danced to it with camp abandon, since, despite my dislike of that orchestra, I couldn't resist a lovely leader's *cabeceo*.

There were unusually few professional dancers at *Cachirulo* last night and, as a result, few people on the floor were dancing with breath-taking elegance. But most people were stepping with precise timing, catching small moments in the music, making clear contrasts between the smooth and the punchy. I was struck by their playful feet, their knowledge of the music, their enjoyment of intricate rhythmic detail and their determination to stamp their own personalities onto the dance. People danced with the confidence that comes of deep familiarity with and great love for the music. Their music. And, by adoption, ours.

Milonga 10 and Divertango

Milonga 10

"This is the most challenging floor in the world," a friend exclaimed, as he was jostled and botty-bumped several times in one D'Arienzo number (at *10*, the leaders take the knocks). Look at the *ronda* and you can certainly get an impression of chaos. But, no matter how crowded it gets, people don't modify their dance. The changes of direction are just as fast, the *boleos* as high, the moves as complex, the *giros* as whirly.

The *pista* as a whole is not a beautiful sight. But the individual dancers are extraordinary. It's rare to spot a beginner there in peak season: the floor is too intimidating for anyone unaccustomed to white-water rafting this complex, fast-moving *ronda*. This is the fast lane of the freeway and you are ill advised to go on it if your car still sports its L-plates.

It's hard to make *mirada/cabeceo* work at *Milonga 10*. The leaders often have an agenda for the evening or at least for the *tanda*. These guys are black belts in the art of ocular self-defence. Rejections take the form of a warm smile as you meet your prospective partner's eyes. Invitations are casual, quick and seemingly nonchalant: "Hey, want to dance this?" The *tanda* selections are classic and everyone knows the music backwards, forwards and inside out. And everyone clears the floor between *tandas* and parts with a peck on the cheek – even if they have only danced one song (beginning mid-*tanda* is common at *10*).

A good night at *10* can feel like heaven and a bad night can leave you wondering whether you still make the grade. A very high proportion of those on the floor are serious dancers. I'm talking mesmerising-to-watch beautiful. The kind of people whose performance videos I watch for inspiration. Get-serious-about-your-dancing-or-fuck-off beautiful.

One thing's for sure, *Milonga 10* is not your ordinary milonga.

Divertango: an antidote to competition style

In the dim blue lighting, on the small tiled floor, the young mostly Argentines danced a crazy, twisty tango. Hovering suspended pauses and sudden bursts of explosive speed abounded; *ochos* were overturned, open male legs were *ganchoed*, female feet flicked through playful decorations. There were no lengthy leg-lines here: legs were bent in whatever ways were necessary to make the movement work. There were no *salony* sequences, no predictable figures. There wasn't time to be even fleetingly aware of grace or elegance. The leads sent me through every twisty position like a human slinky and I listened intently to the music so I could play as hard as my partners, give as good as I got. "This is a refreshing change from the way people danced at the *Metropolitano*," I told my favourite partner. "If I had entered the *Metro*," he said, "I would have been out in the first round." After the sleek sterile aesthetic of the competition, it was like *leaving a fetid, shuttered sick room and coming out into a breezy meadow in May.*

La Marshàll and Queer Tango

The unique atmosphere of La Marshàll

If you overlook the fact that most people on the floor are dancing in same-sex couples, *La Marshàll* (at *El Beso* on Friday nights) is a representative microcosm of the tango world.

There is a small scattering of serious dancers, including, sometimes, a few of the top dancers in the world. Many of them are looking for some floor time dancing in a sex-reversed role. Some are gay and enjoy getting to close embrace someone of their own sex, especially if they spend most of the rest of the week dancing in a traditional sexual configuration.

Then there are the people who dance socially, taking only occasional classes, who perhaps dance 'badly' by the standards of the serious dancers, but are enjoying themselves. There are many beginners. And there are always some people who have never danced tango before and just want to 'give it a go.' Plus some who are not much interested in the dance, but like going to *La Marshàll* because it is a nice evening out, the atmosphere is relaxed, they want to dance a little tango and drink a lot of rum and orange juice and there are many scantily-clad beautiful guys (as well as some cute girls) there, providing an aesthetically-pleasing backdrop.

The floor craft at *La Marshàll* is the worst in Buenos Aires (though, since almost no one wears heels, the *ronda* is less dangerous than it might be). But the atmosphere is perhaps the nicest and warmest I've experienced anywhere. Two groups who are normally quite hostile towards each other – the serious dancer-dancers and the primarily social dancers – coexist there in relaxed harmony.

Queer Eye for the Straight Tango Guy

It was one of those phrases that stays with you forever. We were teenagers looking at a glossy magazine together, one of my oldest gay male friends and I, and one of the ads featured a suave and mysterious looking man in a Burberry trench coat, of a similar build and colouring to my friend. "Oh God," my friend exclaimed with teenage melodrama, "I don't know whether I would prefer to fuck him or be him".

I was reminded of this tonight at *La Marshàll*. Why would you want to dance with another man if you're a straight guy, especially if you live in Buenos Aires and have many excellent female partners to choose from? There is the opportunity to practise the follower's role, of course which is both enjoyable in itself and can help you to improve your own leading by letting you experience what feels good and what feels less pleasurable. But there are other incentives, too.

La Marshàll on a good night is the tango equivalent of *Queer Eye for the Straight Guy*. The best dancers are beautiful and stylish and their dance is prettier, cleaner and more precise, and just *lovelier* than that of most straight boys – it would suit any man. *Hey straight boy, go on, you know you want to wear that well-fitted shirt too. The colour will bring out your eyes! Girls will like it.* If you think you need to look or behave in some clichéd macho way when you are dancing, watch the gay boys with their feline-footed walks and twisty torsos. It looks so right, so well suited to tango. To be a leader, you don't need to be a Man with a capital M. You need to be a dancer.

Secondly, there is the solidarity, comradeship and bromance. There's something thrilling about leading a man, who, while he is as light on his feet, as delicate with his decorations and as soft and responsive as any woman, also knows what it means to lead. As a friend put it: "You are colleagues, you understand each other."

Dancing with another man can give you a sense of what you yourself could and should feel like when dancing.

There are so few occasions on which straight men have affectionate close physical contact with other men. Tango is one of the few opportunities to hold another man in your arms for a sustained period. That gay boy makes you feel amazing in his embrace simply because he is such a great dancer. Even if you would never have sex with another man you have an alternative way of relating physically, a way of getting pleasure from their proximity. That is extremely valuable, especially if you are straight.

I love watching men following from other men. Partly because it's still relatively unusual to see good male following. But mostly because I adore the 'follower's face' they get: eyes closed, lips slightly parted in blissful absorption. I don't often see men make that face. At least, not while dancing tango.

Let's thank our lucky stars for evolutionary biology and the fact that most men will prefer embracing women, all other things being equal. Because, make no mistake, my fellow tangueras, we've got competition. I've seen how my straight male friends look after dancing amazing *tandas* with the best gay boy dancers. The really good dancers don't care if you are wearing a mini skirt. They are chasing the blissful experiences the dance has to offer. You don't dance with your groin. It doesn't matter whether or not you have a penis. There's no tango equivalent of *The Crying Game*. So don't rely on your feminine charms. Go watch those lovely gay boys. Watch and learn.

Pride

LGBT issues have always been close to my heart, not only because gay and trans rights are human rights first and foremost, but because a society without sexual diversity would be deeply impoverished in ways impossible to predict.

The queer and gay milongas have enriched and diversified our tango society. Even if you are straight and have no intention of ever dancing with someone of your own sex or of dancing the other role, I think you would enjoy the atmosphere at *La Marshàll* or *Queer Tango*. These milongas were originally conceived as safe spaces, where anyone could feel comfortable independent of their role, sex, sexuality, sartorial preferences or anatomy. And, while, luckily, these spaces are becoming more plentiful in the Western world, the friendliness and inclusivity at such places can make you feel extremely relaxed. When people of both sexes dance either role, there are so many more possibilities for enjoyment, so many more potential partners and so much more tolerance of learners than usual. Partly because so many people are trying out a role which is not their primary one and at which they may therefore be less skilled. And partly because of the spirit of playful experimentation that these places often foster.

As with all inclusive communities, there are potential drawbacks. Some of my LGBT friends have voiced their frustrations about the relatively low level of dance at some events. There can be more emphasis on socialising and enjoying friendships than on dedicated practice. The personal is often as important as the technical. And, with so many inexperienced leaders out on the *pista*, the floorcraft can be chaotic. But some stunning dancers are regulars, too, particularly among the lithe, balletic, apple-bottomed, jean-clad gay men.

The gay milongas are a haven. A place where rigid rules and traditions are relaxed, where you don't feel like a woman competing with other women, seated in a long row of your same sex peers, all dressed up, made up and kitted out, batting your eyes at the men across the room ("That's what they do at *El Beso* the rest of the week. That's what they consider 'normal,'" Augusto, the host of *La Marshàll*, once quipped). You can stop being painfully aware of the fact that youth and looks are factors in many men's partner choices. You don't have to feel like a woman with a capital W. But you can if you want to and there are no chromosomal prerequisites (though a pair of 8cm tango heels will help).

Whatever your sex, at the queer milonga you will feel like an insider, you'll feel unselfconscious about dancing with whomever you like, in whatever configuration you prefer. As Sabine Ibes puts it, you'll be just "a person, dancing with other people."

It hasn't always been this way. The LGBT community created this – for all of us. Now that's an achievement to be proud of.

The great vibe at La Marshàll

What *La Marshàll* celebrates above all is freedom of partner choice, a value extremely dear to me. There is a genuine openness there towards dancing with people of either sex, in any role, in any combination of ages. You'll see dykey young women with crew cuts leading older milongueras normally seen at the traditional, split-seating milongas; professional dancers in drainpipe jeans leading white-haired men with clumsy steps but blissful smiles; and people of indeterminate sex leading with confidence in vertigo-inducing stripper heels.

Embracing anyone of either sex or in transition between them feels natural here – as I wish it did everywhere. *La Marshàll* is a microcosm of an ideal society and, even if you spend the entire evening dancing only with people of the opposite sex, the liberal, inclusive atmosphere will let you breathe more freely.

It lets you focus on what is important: a way of connecting to people which is sensual, but goes beyond questions of sex and sexuality. *La Marshàll* is a sacred space, a place where our genital configurations, our accidental sex chromosomes, our socially sanctioned gender roles are unimportant. What is important? The worship of the tango gods, for whom we are just convenient vessels.

La Marshàll with an ambitanguera date

For most of the night, my friend and I were the only women among a crowd of young, beautiful-arsed gay men in their drainpipe jeans and black T-shirts. "This song isn't appropriate for *this* milonga," she quipped, as the DJ played "*Llorar por una mujer* ('Crying over a woman')."

I love going to *La Marshàll* with an ambitanguera date, swapping shoes and roles every couple of *tandas*, sufficient unto ourselves, even if none of the pretty boys look in our direction.

I get a thrill when I feel the whipped cream smoothness of her movement, the twistiness of her upper back, her free leg looping through *sacadas* and arcing high into *boleos*. I couldn't decide what I enjoyed more: striding out or *giroing* every which way. I just knew that I didn't want to open the embrace, that it felt fantastic to overturn things, to let the forward *ochos* travel backwards and the back ones forward, to use *sacadas* to get momentum for *boleos*, to loop her around into a series of *paradas* after *paradas*. I felt suddenly powerful, calm, relaxed and grounded and even got a little overconfident when I led the *tanda* of huge instrumental late Puglieses.

What I enjoy most about leading is approaching the music from a different angle, being immersed in the same tango but not in the same way as you are as a follower. Quite apart from the different opportunities this presents musically, you get to witness, feel, sense and sometimes see the follower's musicality from within the embrace but on the other side of it.

At Iguazú falls, most of the waterfalls are on the Argentine side of the border, where you can walk among them, up close and personal. But although there are few waterfalls across on the Brazilian side, it's only from there that you can survey the full panorama. Tonight, I crossed the border and saw the waterfalls from just far enough to appreciate them in their full glory.

The importance of queer tango

I love the difference between the two roles. I love to put on stiletto heels, pretty skirts, perfume and mascara, be held in the arms of an attractive boy and enjoy the playful enactment of heterosexual sensuality which is traditional tango. But our enjoyment in tango is not only about the erotic. Pleasure in music, movement and human proximity is much more complex and multi-faceted than that. Just because I enjoy the traditional sexual configuration doesn't mean I always want to dance like that. It doesn't mean I think it is more 'authentic.' And it certainly doesn't mean I want to prescribe it for everyone.

Which is why I go to *Queer Tango* on a Tuesday night from time to time. For the cute young gay boys dancing with older straight women; the dykey women in flat shoes who don't know how to dance as followers; the beautiful male dancers twisting and pivoting their way through the follower's part of the *giro*; same-sex friends enjoying their walking cuddles; and people equally at ease in both roles. To see how little difference it makes what chromosomes you or your partner possess. What is important is the music, the embrace and the movement – not The Man Woman Thing.

Women leaders in Baires

I've been thinking about the opportunities and problems for women leaders here in Baires. Of course, at all the formal, split-seating milongas it is taboo to dance with someone of your own sex. But those milongas are not the problem. The rules there are crystal clear and they represent only a few out of many local options.

They are our High Church and people go there partly for the bells and incense and many, including me, love them for their mixed-age clientele and because the social aspects of the milonga – the chatting, drinking, schmoozing, small talk and hanging out – are secondary there and the focus is on the dancing.

What's much more significant is how the faithful worship at our many ostensibly relaxed, informal chapels. At most milongas and even *prácticas* you will spot few or no female leaders, even though same-sex couples are definitely *allowed* and no one will bat an eyelid if you *do* get up to dance with a friend who shares your sex chromosomal configuration.

So why doesn't it happen more often? Well, first of all, in our local tango culture, most women will not ask another random woman to dance. Women almost always dance exclusively with their close female friends. This is partly because many women prefer dancing with men or dancing their own role, *all other things being equal,* and therefore have a higher threshold when it comes to the other women they wish to partner. Also, as experienced followers themselves, they know at a visceral level what great following should feel like.

It is also partly fear of encountering a squeamish reaction (these are rare, but once you've had someone squirming in your arms in obvious disgust at the proximity of your boobs you will not want to repeat the experience).

Most of my female friends are highly-skilled dancers accustomed to dancing with excellent male leaders. I don't feel I *should* embrace them unless I can give them an experience of comparable pleasure, which seems like an impossible task. I will never catch up with those talented male dancers who have spent thousands of hours learning their role and have years of experience in the *ronda*. (This is one of many reasons why I strongly advise women to learn both roles from the outset).

54

If you are a female leader coming to visit us in Baires: go to group classes as a leader to find potential partners; wear flat shoes and trousers (visually announcing that you're taking on the traditionally masculine role will help); take a risk on the first few people you ask and get out there, get seen leading – people will quickly catch on that that is your role.

Or look for a regular partner-in-crime, an experienced follower and fellow would-be *ambitanguera* to interchange roles with. But do not let the leading skills you have quietly rust in a corner. I would love to see more female leaders out there dancing. The main thing inhibiting female leading is the simple social cowardice of not wanting to stand out. The main problem is that no one else is doing it. Let's change that.

El Yeite

A tough nut to crack

El Yeite is an excellent psychological training ground to equip you for high-powered, daunting milongas. The place seems almost designed to make it difficult to get dances: with its dim lighting; long, long *cortinas*; louche, lonely, Hopper-esque bar room vibe; unrelentingly dramatic music; frenetic floorcraft – I've seen not a single collision, but many excitingly near misses; slender, peach-fuzzily young women enjoying the privileges of youth; incredibly skilled professionals who seem to own the floor, with their lightning-fast reaction speeds and sheer chutzpah; and all the leaders sitting out many *tandas*, preferring to sip their caipirinhas than to get into the fast lane on that *pista* (there is no slow lane there).

Many of those at *El Yeite* are young professional dancers who have come to have fun swapping partners among each other. This is their off-duty playtime. If you don't get many dances there, don't take it as a judgement on your dancing. There's no time for judgement here; people are too busy squeezing every last drop of pleasure out of their deep, deep late-night tango.

The dancing has special drama – both in terms of amplitude of movement – with bodies spiralling tightly, free legs flying, embrace distances changing elastically – and of musicality – swoopy dramatic pauses, sudden explosive accelerations and very emphatic use of syncopation – as befits the late-night hour, the intense music (lots of Troilo and Pugliese) and all the big swirly movement happening on the floor.

All those things combine to make *El Yeite* one of the most difficult places in the world to get dances. Adjust your expectations accordingly. Go with friends – or be ready to just sit back and enjoy the show. This is not your ordinary neighbourhood milonga. But when you *do* have great *tandas* at *The Secret Club* (my translation), you'll feel like humming that old Sinatra tune: "if you can make it there, you'll make it anywhere."

The plebs take over El Yeite

It's official. The plebs took over *El Yeite* last night. Many of the glamorous professionals are on tour at the moment, leaving only a scattering of those sleek pussycats and plenty of space for us mice to play. It feels almost like a normal milonga – no, I take that back; I *wish* this were the norm. I danced *tanda* after *tanda* of the intense *Yeitian* music until well after rosy fingers smeared the sky over Avenida Córdoba, until the sky was the watercolour blue of early morning, and it was light enough to make my sequinned top and eyeliner feel like the tell-tale trappings of a walk of shame. Until my coach turned back into a pumpkin, or rather into the crimson-eyed 168 bus, which took me past a Plaza Once campily decked out in a profusion of pale violet *jacarandá* flowers.

Now I'm home, smeary eyed and thirsty, as a bright blue late spring day is beginning. Through the thin walls of my flat, I can hear my neighbours' alarm clock beeping. It's time for Muggles to get up and stumble to the shower to start the preparations for the day. Good night, my friends!

The manic-depressive madness of El Yeite

As a friend remarked last night: "*El Yeite* is the both the best and the worst place to dance in Buenos Aires."

It's a truly manic-depressive place. The standard of social dancing on a good night is surely the highest to be found anywhere. But, if you're not a pretty confident leader, you shouldn't be out on that floor at all, just as you wouldn't go down a double black diamond ski run as a novice. And, if you're not an excellent follower, you won't get dances, unless you are exceptionally young and beautiful.

To judge if, as a follower, you are ready for *El Yeite*, ask yourself: would you feel confident if, unexpectedly, Sebastian Arce, Chicho or the idol of your choice asked you to dance a pretty fast set of Biagi valses and pulled out all the stops. If you know you would be nervous about following that, you're *not* ready for *El Yeite*. If you would be thrilled and delighted and are pretty sure Sebastian, Chicho, etc. would really enjoy dancing with you, well, you're either deluded or you *are* ready.

But, even if you are a really good dancer, pretty confident that those on the floor – or, at least, a good proportion of them – are your peers, you still might spend the whole night on your arse. Be warned. *El Yeite* is surely the most difficult scene to break into anywhere. If you are the kind of person who worries about 'cliques' and 'snobs,' you will hate it. And, even if you love the place, it won't necessarily love you back.

La Viruta

Social observations on La Viruta

I am not, in general, fond of *schmooze-eceo* or *chat-eceo*. But an approach of that kind works well at that exceptionally dark and crowded milonga, *La Viruta*: a *porteño* Noah's ark on Friday and Saturday nights after 3.30am, with animals of every species on the dance floor, two by two – though very good dancers tend to predominate due to floor craft Malthusianism. (This is not a place where you will survive long as a leader without a black belt in navigation).

The lighting and room layout make long-range *cabeceo* impossible. So, usually, I circulate and greet acquaintances and gauge their reactions. Some grab me and take me out on the floor instantly, or as soon as a new *tanda* begins. Others chat, hug, say "*ah*, it's lovely to see you" and then edge away discreetly.

There is frequently an inverse relationship between how warmly people greet me and how much they would like to dance with me – the warmth is designed to both cover and make up for the lack of desire to dance. And then there are those who let the conversation peter out but remain there next to me, hovering, eyes on the dance floor, saying nothing. I usually shoot them a meaningful look at point blank range or sometimes ask "feel like dancing to this?" Hovering around next to someone, especially in an awkward, liminal spot, is a universal sign of being open to the idea of dancing with them and this is one of the few situations in which asking men to dance usually pays off.

However, how people who don't know anyone there get dances with the better dancers at *La Viru* remains a complete mystery to me.

Baires Festivals

Festivals in Buenos Aires

In the States, for many, the main draw of a festival is the opportunity to dance with a much wider range of people than they can locally. For some, it's about being able to dance with more partners at a higher level than their home scene can offer, while others look forward to being reunited with their favourite partners who live scattered around the country. The presence of well-known *maestros* is an additional attraction, but, for a lot of festival-goers, classes and performances are of secondary importance and many people even complain that the exhibitions take away good dancing time. Many people are a lot more anxious to know who the DJs will be than what classes are on offer.

Here in Baires, it's the other way round. A festival here is a smorgasbord of group classes and seminars, given mostly by dancers at the very top level of their profession, extremely well-informed about the body's biomechanics and how to make movements more fluid and efficient. The classes are usually much longer than regular group lessons, running sometimes to three or four hours. (Unlike classes in the US, they are likely to start at least thirty minutes late, a phenomenon on which many sleepy headed late risers rely). They are often at least twice as expensive as regular classes per hour, though still cheap by first-world standards. Attendance is higher, too. Regular classes, even by the best teachers, can be spottily attended here because of the wealth of lessons on offer. I've had a lot of accidental semi-private lessons and I've lost count of the number of teachers who've cancelled classes because of low turnout. It doesn't help that the locals are often very bad at advertising: there is no reliable, easily-accessible and clear guide to classes in Buenos Aires and online information is frequently out of date. But, at a festival, you can generally guarantee that the class will be packed. And, unlike in the States, where most class attendees are not very highly skilled dancers and advanced level is often a euphemism for beginner/intermediate (the teachers themselves are often the only advanced level dancers at the festival), here in Baires, advanced level means precisely that. They aren't joking. (I'm always especially thrilled to see some of my favourite dancers attending class themselves).

As for the festival milongas, many locals will be unaware of or uninterested in their existence and won't be drawn away from their local circuit. Both *Cachirulo* and *El Beso* were buzzing this weekend, with all my favourite regulars were in attendance, despite the fact that they clashed with the closing events of the Misterio Tango Festival.

But if you think the festival milongas aren't full to bursting, you are mistaken. They are wholly unlike festival milongas in the US. They are *seriously* crowded. Chairs are slotted so tightly together that to move involves a complex process of getting a dozen people to each shift a tiny fraction, like a living puzzle box in which you can only slide one counter at a time. Out on the floor, at peak hours, the *tanda* is spent dancing a thousand *ocho cortados* in succession, trying to distil the drama of a Pugliese or the high energy of a D'Arienzo down into the tiniest gestures, smallest decorations and subtlest differences in how you step or change weight. Many of the better leaders wait hours, talking in shouted conversations over the painfully loud music, until later in the evening, when they finally dance on the somewhat thinned-out *pista* of 4 or 5am.

And I haven't even mentioned the shows yet. There are the old maestros, a little bent, hunched or blubbery, not as athletic or elegant anymore, but still eliciting warm cheers because we watch them not

59

for what they show on the outside but for what they represent and embody: a link with tradition, a tribute to decades serving the tango. And then there are the beautiful young people: improvised *salon*y performances of breath-taking smoothness alternate with an unusual proportion of choreographies alive with daring moves and dramatic music. Seeing them from close up is a completely different experience from watching them on YouTube. The expectations of the crowd, coupled with the sight of every tiny mistake – an ankle trembling for balance *here*, a back *sacada* just a millimetre off the ideal *there* – can create an atmosphere that feels more like watching snowboarding than dance.

I have mixed feelings about festivals. I love crowds because of what they mean: lots of visitors means a transfusion of funds and enthusiasm. I don't find it ideal to dance in a *very* packed space, but I love it when a place is still buzzing with tango energy as the sun comes up. The classes can be wonderful – though also pricey and tiring. But I find it stimulating to be among so many people studying hard.

The one thing I don't feel ambivalent about is the performances. I find them inspiring. I don't try to reproduce the more flamboyant decorations or want to be airborne. I'm not an *escenario* dancer. But seeing so many people dancing so well lights a fire under my arse. "I wasn't prepared," a friend told me, "for how beautiful Moira Castellano's walk is. I'm still recovering".

Milonga Culture in the Diaspora

What it's like to go to a diaspora milonga where you only enjoy dancing with one or two partners

No one likes to feel pressurised into having to dance with someone and some people are more sensitive to these pressures than others. This can quickly add a layer of social awkwardness in tango scenes, where, either because of their small size or your own choosiness about partners, people you enjoy dancing with are a scarcity.

This is especially true if travel to and from milongas is complicated or expensive, if getting home in the early morning hours afterwards involves a long dark walk from a bus stop in a rough neighbourhood or if money is tight and you are doing complicated mental calculations to work out whether you can pay the entrance fee and wondering whether you can surreptitiously swig from your sports bottle of water, since drinks are so expensive there. In that situation, I'm guessing that this interior monologue is common:

"Will *Twinkletoes* and *Twisty* be there? If they are both there, they will probably each dance with me, at least one *tanda*, perhaps two. Are the costs in time and money worth it for a probable maximum of four *tandas*? What if only *Twinkletoes* is there? There are a lot of women he likes dancing with: will I get a *tanda* with him? Is it worth going on the off-chance of just one *tanda*? *Twisty* sometimes dances a lot and sometimes prefers to spend the evening mostly drinking and socialising. Is it worth going to the milonga just for the chance of dancing with him, knowing I might not get to dance at all?" Many dancers have told me that they make these kinds of mental calculations. Sometimes it's unavoidably obvious when you've come to the milonga just to dance with a few specific people. This dependency that can make me feel exceptionally uncomfortable. It's the kind of feeling which can make me stay at home. So, when you *know* that *Twinkletoes* and *Twisty* have come to the milonga for you just as much as vice versa, you can feel a huge sense of relief ("thank goodness, they like dancing with me too, it's mutual! It's not just me being needy!") and you may give them big hugs, smile and chat and feel like friends.

But it isn't because they are 'in your clique' that you dance with them. It isn't because you are friends that you seek them out or because you are excluding others or are socially snobby (*ah!* if *only* there were a few new, exciting, unknown partners for you). It's because it's hard to hate someone who enables you to share an experience of intense pleasure with them or who has just turned your evening from one of sitting with a glass of wine and twitchy legs longing to dance to one of tango bliss. If you feel that the good dancers are cliquey, think about this.

La Milonga Porteña in Rovigo

I am often told "our milonga is just like a traditional Buenos Aires milonga" but I'd never found one that actually seemed that

61

way, until I visited *La Milonga Porteña* in Rovigo. The only things missing to make it seem completely like *Cachirulo* were waitress service and the host Hector, who has not yet discovered that microphones amplify sound, shouting fit to bust everyone's eardrums. But we had split seating, with men and women on different long sides of the room (and a couples' section across the short side); alcoholic drinks and syrupy espressos at the well-stocked bar (I like to balance out my uppers and downers); assigned tables and cross-room *cabeceo*.

The men walked over and collected the women from their chairs and brought us back to our seats at the end of the *tanda*, clearing the floor completely during the *cortina*. No one danced consecutive *tandas*. No one asked for dances verbally. It was a little haven of traditionalist heaven in the Italian *campagna*. I gather the organiser fought against much resistance to create and maintain that old-fashioned ambience. Everything about the place, from the beautiful sprung floor to the *fileteado* lettering over the bar, bore witness to the most loving care.

I love split seating because it highlights the gender dimorphism of tango. My dance — and I — are very girly. I don't mirror the man's movements in a dance of symmetrical androgyny, but for every step of no-nonsense masculine plainness of his, I add a dozen whirls, curls, taps and strokes of my high-heeled free leg while my silky *Poema* skirts fly around in my wake like a gauzy tail.

And I do wish that at traditional milongas in Buenos Aires we also hung around at the bar together at the end of the night, drinking delicious wine and eating slices of local salami.

Elisabetta, mi piace la tua milonga.

The Italian face

There is a lot of very sensual dancing on the Bologna-Rimini-Modena-Rovigo-Ferrara-Venice circuit. As a friend puts it, "the Italians are not afraid to embrace a woman." Almost no one has the caved-in-almost-but-not-quite-touching syndrome and embraces err on the too squeezy, not the too loose, side. People adjust the embrace with stroking, back-caressing movements. They hold the final poses of the songs for a few seconds longer than average. Sometimes they remain in the embrace with me between songs, allowing us to feeling each other's tummies move with our breath. Perhaps they just recognise me for the floozy I am and know that I will love it.

I find myself not resisting "that face" anymore when I feel my brow wanting to furrow a little and my lips to open just a tiny bit. I know it's happening, I'm making the much maligned "orgasm face" of the so-called "overly-sensual follower."

But this is Italy. It feels as natural as throwing my arms high into the air and squealing with pleasure before hugging friends, making loud smacking kissy-kissy noises at babies and saying *mmm mmm mmm* as a mouthful of *burrata* melts creamily on my tongue. I've always disliked the sour judgementalism of onlookers. I don't want to police my facial expressions or curb my natural impulses for their pleasure. Italy is turning me into a "too sensual" follower – and that makes me happy. I'd like us to rename the "orgasm face" the *Italian* face. And I'd like more people to get in touch with their inner Italians.

The Multiple Tangasms milonga
At La Maquina Tanguera, Rimini

There's more than one way to put the music together for the evening. On this night in Rimini, the DJ spun a mellow selection of 80% *Guardia vieja* and only 20% Golden Age – something you'd never hear in Baires. But did this mean that the public danced very simply and plainly? Not at all. The dancing was high energy, twisty and loopy, rich with *boleos, ganchos* and *paradas,* and all in a flexible but sustained close embrace, chests touching throughout, no matter what. It was Carlitos-and-Noelia style, *milonguero* style on speed.

During those slow Canaros, OTVs and Lomutos, there was plenty of time for the men to catch triplets, off beats and subtle rhythmic variations and for me to decorate so much it no longer felt like *adornos* but like an intrinsic part of the quality of my movement.

But what I liked best were the embraces. The men's right arms wrapped around me without squeezing or gripping. Their hands touched me lightly and their left arms were soft as *gelato,* lighter than the froth on a *caffè shakerato*.[2] But they were fully present: I felt their upper bodies clearly and firmly against mine from chest to tummy. They embraced me as though they meant it, as though they enjoyed

---

[2] iced, blended espresso, sometimes served with sugar syrup

my female body close to theirs – and almost everyone held me in the embrace between songs and even between *tandas* on a few occasions.

Looking out of the window, the shimmering reflections in the glass made it seem as if we were dancing on the surface of the sea. What a night!

Some Milonga Fauna

Bottom Feeders

Our tango scene here in Buenos Aires provides a rich and diverse ecosystem in which many different life forms find their ecological niches. When the place is packed with visitors, it affects the predator-prey balance. Our indigenous fauna inevitably include bottom-feeding scavengers. It's all about suitable environments and convergent evolution. Just as a crowded gathering will draw pickpockets, a crowded milonga with many innocent newcomers will draw bottom feeders.

Their natural habitat is semi-formal milongas (i.e. milongas where people tend to dress up, are allocated tables when they enter, order drinks from waiters, etc. but don't have split seating by sex). They abound at *Canning* and lurk in the obscurity of *La Viruta* (they love skulking in dark corners, preparing their ambushes). They avoid places where men and women are largely segregated and it's more difficult to make a direct approach to your prey. Their prey animals are foreign women, first-time visitors to Buenos Aires, often older women from diaspora scenes in which everyone is friendly and accommodating, it's considered impolite to decline a dance and breaking *tanda* would be a scandal. If they see a face that looks unfamiliar, it's fair game.

They prefer beginner dancers, since they are less quick to recognise that what they are doing most certainly *isn't* tango. They generally prefer to ask for dances verbally, carefully seeking out the innocent and searching for unfamiliar faces. Because if they *do* accidentally ask someone who has been around the local *ronda* a few times, the response will be rolled eyes and a look of utter disdain.

Once they have the woman in their sweaty grasp, they begin the gradual process of preparing their prey for consumption. It starts with a little extra squeeze or two, a gentle caress of the spine, a sigh at the beauty of these lovely Di Sarlis, an arm that snakes around the waist and, if you let them, things might then escalate to *extra* close *paradas* in which you may feel things standing to attention that shouldn't be, to alcoholic fumes in your face and even the odd slobber at the corner of your lips (careful: these beasts carry a lot of germs).

If you are a newcomer to Baires, keep an eye out for bottom feeders. When you enter a new milonga, observe the dancers for a while before accepting any invitations. If it's a formal place, say a polite "no, thank you" to anyone who approaches and asks you to dance at your table. (You may see other women leaping up happily at verbal invitations – but almost always in response regular partners they know well, not random strangers.) Seek out and accept your dances by *mirada/cabeceo*. If you can, ask your female table mates for advice and recommendations.

Once you're out on the floor, trust your instincts. It's acceptable here to be very *verbally* flirtatious, to give charming compliments between songs, to ask "are all the women in Topeka as beautiful as you?" But it's not normal to stroke the woman's back (*ewwww*), inch your hand round to her side boob, stick a pair of blubbery lips in her face or do anything that brings her into intentional contact with your groin. Also, remember that dancing is voluntary, especially if you feel creeped out, if you're thinking "ugh, I don't like this, but there's a small chance he grabbed my nipple by accident, I'm not 100% sure, I don't want to be unfair on him, maybe he always caresses the woman's arse during Caló numbers, maybe his fingers are unconsciously echoing the piano, maybe he's just being 'Latin.'" You are not about to take the person to court or confine them to the stocks. You don't need to prove anything to anyone beyond reasonable doubt. It's enough that *you* feel uncomfortable. Exit the situation. Get out of Dodge. Decline to dance, break *tanda* (mid-song if necessary), warn your friends. Once, I had even already accepted a dance when I spotted a friend making unmistakable signals that the man in question was a bottom feeder, repeatedly miming the slitting of her own throat and shaking her head with increasing urgency. So I said "um, sorry, actually, I've changed my mind, I don't want to dance after all."

Please don't worry about 'causing a scene'. No one will think the worse of you for breaking *tanda* with a creep. Quite the contrary. Many of these guys are already notorious.

And watch out for the most insidious bottom feeder of all: the kind who teaches tango. Occasionally, a handsome, elegant teacher, perhaps even someone you have watched admiringly in a thousand YouTube videos, will moonlight as a bottom feeder. While he will behave himself with partners he respects, he thinks that *you* will be so thrilled to be in his arms that you'll be willing to put up with just about anything. Sisters, please. Prove him wrong.

I apologise for our bottom feeders. There are only a few of them, relatively speaking. But, if you are their classic prey, you may find yourself repeatedly singled out. My female friends, stay safe. Operate a zero tolerance policy. And, men, if you witness or hear about this, point out those guys and warn your female acquaintances.

Desperados

I think we've all encountered those men: the ones who come up and stand at a distance of 20cm from your chair, silently staring or thrusting out a hand; the ones who tap you on the shoulder when you are deep in conversation; who block your path when you try to walk to the bar or ambush you at the door of the ladies' toilet as you exit; who grab you by the biceps and pull gently but firmly in the direction of the dance floor; who demand an explanation for your polite "no, thanks" or even mutter "bitch" at your refusal.

My working hypothesis is that these are men who have become embittered by trying milder methods and receiving many refusals. But being so rude and aggressive is like wearing a T shirt announcing "No woman would dance with me, except under extreme duress. So here I am to try to force you." This is not an announcement it is politic to make if you would like people to dance with you. As a result, they have even less success and resort to even more violent methods in an eternal vicious circle.

Feel free to say "no, thanks" to any man (or woman) who asks in a rude or demanding way. People will think you are very sensible to refuse them and, if you accept, they will pity you. And don't worry about being called a bitch. Everyone knows that "she's a bitch" is often code for "that woman declined to dance with me." If you decline these guys, the only thing that will happen is that you won't get to dance with someone you wouldn't have wanted to dance with anyway. And perhaps they will gradually learn that aggression isn't a great strategy for getting dances.

The Mercuries

There's a category of men at the milonga I call The Mercuries, since they switch so easily from signalling warmth to coolness. On a smaller scale, there are guys who dance with me multiple times one week and then look at me with total disinterest the next and then *cabeceo* me again eagerly and happily the following week, etc. (though in a less predictable pattern than this). There are guys who dance with me multiple times every time we coincide at a milonga, for months on end, and then suddenly avoid my gaze. Some of them return to dancing with me on a regular basis at a later stage and there are even a few with whom this cycle has repeated itself more than once. And some, suddenly, without warning, decide never to dance with me again.

It's very easy to get paranoid about this behaviour. Several things help to diffuse this paranoia: one is that I've rarely perceived any personal animosity from Mercuries; another is the knowledge that there are many factors involved in partner choice, some of which may have nothing whatsoever to do with me personally; and a third reassuring thing is that I have heard the same story from *many* of my friends. Mercuries abound in tango, particularly in Buenos Aires. Just stay calm, don't take it personally, don't bear grudges (I'm ready to dance with Mercuries when the silver fluid starts rising again) and, as always, don't fixate on those who, for whatever reason, currently don't dance with you. Enjoy those who do.

Advice for Beginners

Increasing your chances of getting dances as a beginner leader:
some tips

1. Put on a crisp white shirt (dressing well will make some people give you the benefit of the doubt). Be prepared to get lipstick on that shirt if you are very tall and want to dance with shorter followers. Lipstick marks on a tall man's tango shirt at breast level are the honourable battle scars of the *pista*.

2. Choose your milonga carefully. Avoid places that are very crowded or full of high-level dancers. If you find yourself at such a place, chill out, order a glass of wine and settle down to spend an evening listening to the music and watching. If you're seated next to someone who seems friendly, ask them if they know what orchestra is playing. It's a good way to learn to recognise the different orchestras.

3. Go early, before the milonga becomes crowded.

4. Observe people's behaviour for a while before you decide how and whether to seek dances. If in doubt, always use *cabeceo*. Get those peepers working and, if necessary, fake a confidence you don't feel.

5. Choose music you are familiar with, if you can. Avoid dramatic or fast music. If you're not sure whether it's tango, waltz or milonga, sit out that *tanda*.

6. When you're out on the floor, keep things *really* simple. Simpler than you think. *Much* simpler. Just walk and lead *ocho cortados*. Under no circumstances lead a *gancho* or *volcada*.

7. If you are off balance, loosen the embrace and pause to recuperate. If *she's* off balance, loosen the embrace and let her find her own balance. If things are a bit wobbly, loosen the embrace. Don't grip or squeeze. Stay gentle and soft. Being a collection of strands of loosey goosey wet spaghetti is preferable to hurting someone. (If you're a stick of wobbly butter, she'll just dance around you, but if you hold her with a grip of steel, she'll be miserable). Anything you do to try to help the follower with her movements is overwhelmingly likely to hinder her instead.

8. If she decorates, enjoy it. She's paying you a big compliment by being willing to have fun with you. More musical followers often use decorations to demonstrate how they hear the music.

9. If you find that you are bumping into a lot of people, even if you think it's not your 'fault,' you may need to go back to lessons and the *práctica* for a little longer. Meanwhile, watch how the other guys manage the floor space and ask your teachers to focus on floorcraft.

10. If she breaks *tanda*, don't get offended. It's probably for your own safety.

11. Understand that it's risky for a follower to dance with a beginner who may not have mastered the art of navigating the *pista*. It's easy for her to get injured. It's therefore normal to hear "no, thanks." It's not personal and it doesn't mean that you will never be a good dancer. Let the good dancers you see inspire you. Chat to the other men and ask them for tips. Remember that time spent at the milonga just listening to the music and observing is not time wasted. Don't get bitter or resentful and, if you start feeling unhappy, go home.

Fear of the milonga

Dear Terpsi,

I am a five months beginner and it takes all that I have within me to go to milongas and even *prácticas*. If I am feeling any weakness physical or emotional, I can't dredge up the emotional fortitude to go. Once there, I usually have a good time, though I know my partners can feel my anxiety and tension, as I have not yet learned to relax.

Love, Nervous Beginner

Dear Nervous,

I remember how it feels to have performance anxiety when dancing socially. The only way to get past it is to go out dancing as much as you can, so you can first get used to the feeling and then, eventually, it will disappear.

In the meantime, here's what helped me.

Try to look for partners among other beginners. Ask around in classes and see where they go and when. Beginner leaders usually go to the milonga early (floor craft is often challenging later, when the milonga fills up), so show up right when it starts. And, if there is a pre-milonga class, go. It's a good way to warm up.

When you're actually dancing, try to focus on the music and your partner. Don't worry about how you make your partner feel – think about how he (or she) makes you feel. Remember that neither you nor they are there to practise, but to dance and enjoy.

Don't apologise for your dancing. If something goes wrong, laugh it off. The important thing will be the overall experience of the dance. Individual mistakes, missed leads, etc. happen to everyone, even the most experienced, and are *really* unimportant.

Having too much tension in the body is very common for beginners. Your body will relax in time. Meanwhile, stretching or yoga can help. Try to visualise yourself embracing the leader in a way that is as close to a soft, melty hug as is compatible with tango. Wearing lower heeled shoes can help with tension in the legs: save the really high, spindly stilettos for when you have more dance experience.

Good luck!

What to do if you're an anxious beginner in the arms of someone who outclasses you

First of all, for maximum dance happiness, it's important to know your level and find milongas and *prácticas* with less experienced or choosy partners and a less daunting atmosphere. Sally Townsend Blake calls this "finding your happy tango." However, sometimes you still might find yourself in the arms of someone whose skill level is way above your own.

If you are a leader, keep things as simple as possible, especially with a more advanced follower – only lead those moves which you have thoroughly mastered. If you want to impress her, do so with your musicality and the softness of your embrace (if in doubt, be gentler than normal, never more forceful).

As a follower, you don't have the option of keeping it simple. Suddenly, he is whirling you through a thousand fast *giros*, you are stumbling, tripping and spiking yourself in your own foot and feel a bit like Miss Piggy in a spin dryer. Or he is dancing slowly, giving you time to notice every wobble and you are trembly and sweaty with the effort of trying to "just relax and follow!" And all the time you are thinking "I've blown it. He will NEVER ask me to dance again. In fact, before I come to this milonga again – which will be not before 2045 – I will have to have major facial plastic surgery or don a *niqab*, since my disgraces on the dance floor tonight will surely go down in history for ever."

I know it's difficult but never apologise for being a beginner. Your partners will quickly notice that you have been dancing for only a short time and any sensible person knows that that means that you will misread leads, get overly tense, stumble here and there, get confused, feel a little shaky. And, in their minds, you will be not be "that *terrible* dancer" but "that *beginner* dancer."

As far as you can, stop worrying about what they must be thinking of your dancing and try to focus on the music and how their dance feels. Do your best to enjoy your partner, as if he (or she) were a delicious ice cream – an ice cream which *licks back*.

A friend of mine always recommends potential dance partners this way: "I think you could get a lot of pleasure out of him." That is the attitude you need. You're dancing with the hot shot, try to get pleasure out of him! And, if not, hold your head high and never apologise for being who you are as a dancer, at that moment.

We've all been there, after all.

How will you get better if the better dancers don't dance with you?

It's one of the most frequent questions I receive: "How can I possibly get better if the best local dancers won't dance with me?"

I'm sceptical of how much you can learn dancing socially with much better dancers but there *are* some things you can learn right away: how soft and relaxed and gentle great dancers feel can be an important revelation. This might make you realise that the dance doesn't require as much tension or resistance as you thought.

If you're a leader, you might also notice how much more advanced followers play with the music and how little assistance they need (usually none) to dance their movements. You might have second thoughts about those bone-clashing shallow *ganchos*, chiropractic back *boleo* leads and straightjacket preparations for forward *ocho* when you find the more advanced followers rooted to the spot refusing to follow you. If something goes wrong in the dance, you know you led it badly and will have to rethink what you're doing, rather than wondering if it was your partner's fault.

If you're a follower, however, it's more difficult to recognise your own failings when dancing with a highly skilled leader. You might be floating along, eyes closed, in a dream world, as he steers your heavy, passive form around the room, wearing a strained half smile to mask his suffering. But then again, dancing with a better dancer may give you an opportunity to respond to movements led out of their usual sequence, free from the beginner leaders' predictable rote-learned patterns, so that you are forced to react rather than second-guessing what is wanted.

If you're really paying attention, you *can* learn some things from your more skilled partner. You can realise that you are doing some things very wrong. And you can get a slight sense of what to aspire to. (I say slight, because you really can't get a sense of how someone's dance feels unless you can give as good as you get – the dance isn't something the other person has on them and can give you some of. It's more like you bringing the raw eggs and them bringing the flour and sugar and then baking the cake together. It's something you create *as a couple*).

These glimpses into the world of the more skilled dancer are no substitute for a real learning experience. What you probably *won't* learn: how to hold your body, transfer weight, dissociate, keep your balance, be grounded, move efficiently, express the music – almost all the fundamentals. You might be able to learn something about which leads work and how to respond to leads as a follower: but leading or following alone isn't dancing. You also have to manage *your own* movement.

So how *do* you get better? Take group classes. Take private lessons. Find a practice partner. If no one of the opposite role is available, consider learning the other role and finding a same-sex (or same-role) partner to switch off with. Practise solo. Go to solo technique classes. Do simple exercises in your kitchen in socks. Get a group of friends together and start a *práctica*. Invite your local teachers to act as guides and mentors (reimburse them for their time and effort, if necessary). Always practise in a careful, conscious way, asking yourself "why am I doing things this way? What am I trying to achieve and is it working?" Don't just repeat things mindlessly or stick to a technique because someone once said it should be done that way. Listen to the music a lot, one orchestra at a time. I recommend singing along to it. Read Michael Lavocah's and Joaquin Amenábar's books on tango music. Read the lyrics to increase your emotional connection with tango culture (if you need translations you can find some at *Poesía de gotán: The Poetry of the Tango*).[3] Dance to the music on your own at home. Do yoga, Pilates, Alexander technique, gyrotonics, Feldenkrais or any other form of bodywork to make your body more flexible and develop proprioception.

Above all, learn to enjoy dancing with people at the same stage in the journey. They are imperfect. But that night when you only dance with people who are 100% flawless will never come. Those partners do not exist. Learn to appreciate *this* person's soft and sensual embrace and *that* person's playful musicality. Learn to enjoy dancing with people who enjoy dancing with you! That's one skill you will need throughout your tango life.

I've danced with some very high-powered dancers. It felt wonderful. But the real learning didn't come from dancing with the stars. It came from explicit verbal feedback from teachers, conscious and careful solo practice and many hours of working with practice partners who were my peers.

That's the real deal, my friends. Stop begging for a taste of someone else's cupcake. Stop trying to figure out the recipe by licking the icing. Get a proper recipe book and get your arse into the kitchen and bake your own.

How much can you learn from dancing with beginners?

It's complex.

First of all, the more people you enjoy dancing with the greater your potential happiness. Being able to compensate for the mistakes of poor dancers is therefore a life-enriching skill. If you can still enjoy the feeling of hugging someone and happily playing in the music together, even if they force you to take your forward *ocho* as a blocky

---

[3] https://poesiadegotan.com/

73

step, or make your right arm ache a little because of excess tension, then you have increased your potential capacity for tango joy. This is particularly wonderful if you are fond of the guy or girl and *want* to learn to love their dance because you love them.

But that's not the same as improving the quality of *your own dance*. In most respects, I've always found it easier – in the sense of less challenging – to dance with leaders less far along in their tango journey. They employ fewer changes of velocity and dance more slowly altogether (though they don't usually employ the extreme slowness which can be its own challenge) and they have less vocabulary. I have more time to respond. They are easier to predict because they use more repeated patterns and habitual ways of moving.

Sometimes you have to compensate for things they are doing wrong, respond to what they *meant* to say, rather than what they said (a following-by-guessing which is not involved in higher level dancing). This isn't always easy. But it is a specific skill. It feels very different from learning to respond sensitively to every nuance of what and how a skilled dancer is leading.

Learning to keep your own balance is not the same as learning how to plant yourself firmly and resist being pushed or pulled. For me, the former is more difficult. I've encountered very few leaders forceful enough to pull me off axis. But I can throw *myself* off balance easily if I don't take each step with precision and care – even if I'm dancing with the most beautiful dancer in the world.

There are times when the other person's technical weaknesses can be actively beneficial. My partner *The Slow Semite* and I often seek out specific *giros* in which he, *enrosque*-d precariously stork-like on one leg, is particularly unstable. Because *I* need to practise placing my steps with geometric precision in order not to compromise his axis. The wobblier he is the better, since it highlights each time I step outside the perfect circle, when my *valediction no longer forbids mourning*. I believe his teacher, *The Master of Calm*, by contrast, would remain on perfect balance in the centre of any *giro* even if you shot him.

However, in many other regards, teachers can be more difficult to dance with than their students: more fun, but more challenging: more creative and therefore fuller of surprises. The clean definition of a really good leader's dance can make me hyperaware of the quality of my movement, including its shortcomings. It's like looking at a painting hung on a pristine white wall. To stay with a great leader, to dance *well* with him, I need to bring my A game.

I want to learn how to *enjoy* dancing with as many people as possible, which means not becoming distracted or thrown off by their technical problems. I don't want to be a princess wriggling uncomfortably on every pea.

But I also want to up my tango game. And that requires being challenged and stretched, having to respond to subtler signals. That's a different skill altogether.

Partner Choice

Never was there a saying that was so apt for the milonga. I generally recite it silently like a mantra at the beginning of at least two or three *tandas* each evening. "If you can't be with the one you love, love the one you're with."

* * *

"We have to keep improving our dance, not for ourselves but for those who dance with us, so that they feel happier."
(A friend, my translation.)

* * *

Almost every good dancer I know would rather sit than suffer through a *tanda* in the arms of a partner whose dancing they cannot enjoy. Acknowledging this would make life in the tango world easier for everyone concerned.

* * *

Many people would benefit from obsessing less about how to 'get' great dances and focusing more on how to give them.

* * *

Partner choice, the milonga environment and our dependence on others

The milonga is a miniature society, a Leviathan in tadpole form, a low-stakes practice game to prepare us for the more hazardous gambles of real life. We need other people for our fulfilment. We can't dance – or spend our lives – alone. Many of us have one overriding desire: to dance with the people who give us the most pleasure. But those other people have their own priorities and there is no easy way to force them to serve our needs.

We have two basic options. There is the big bad wolf approach: huffing and puffing about cliques, snobs, choosy women and arrogant boys, whinging and complaining, attempting to pressurise, bully or guilt-trip, slinging accusations of lookism, ageism or favouritism of all kinds, envy, sulky resentment, and complaining "it's not fair."

Or you can attempt to offer something others will want to choose freely. You can focus on being as good a partner as you can, keep a positive attitude and acknowledge that you simply can't win them all.

Your life does not depend on getting the next *tanda*. You will be perfectly fine if you don't dance those Di Sarlis with *The Enrosque Emperor*. If you cannot cope with *his* blank-eyed lack of response to your longing *mirada*, with *her* no thanks when you gingerly request a *tanda*, how will you ever deal with being made redundant from the job whose income you so badly need, being left by the wife you were so much in love with or hearing the doctor pronounce the cancer diagnosis?

The milonga is the practice run, the dry ski slope, the shallow end of the pool. You can use it as a training ground for self-development. It's your choice.

How I choose partners: the dance is the thing

A lot of the resentments about people's partner choices have to do with an inability to see tango as anything other than a social activity and therefore a belief that the partner choices people make must be primarily related to social questions such as hierarchies, cliques, status anxieties etc.

When I hear those kinds of accusations I often think: you haven't gone very deep into tango; you haven't realised how *different* the experience of dancing can feel with one person than with another. Therefore you are searching for social reasons to explain partner choices.

But, in fact, it's not about social hierarches at all. It's about the dance itself.

If I choose to dance with X, it's because of the experience we can create together. Not because he (or she) is a famous dancer, or the visiting teacher, or particularly sexy, or will make me look good, or is in my clique (though, all other things being equal, I will *definitely* be more inclined to dance with someone I am personally fond of).

It's because I suspect from watching or know from dancing with him (or her) that our shared experience is likely to be an enriching one, in dance terms. That it will feel good to hold him and move together and that I will be able to express what I feel about the music with him and listen to how he feels.

It's as a *dancer* I am making those choices. And what I'm looking for at that moment isn't social validation, it isn't to 'show off,' look good or gain brownie points with the 'in' crowd.

It's because of the *dance*. The dance is the thing.

The most inviting look

The most inviting *cabeceo* of all is when I get the sensation that someone would specifically like to dance with *me*, when instead of scanning the room with a look of hungry desperation in his eyes, trying unsuccessfully to get the attention of a number of different women, a leader looks straight at me with a half-smile and a flirtatious twinkle that says "I've been watching you, my friend, and, you know, I think we would enjoy each other."

Dancing and xenophobia

"Very few of the women will dance with me because I don't look Argentine. Other foreigners don't want to dance with a fellow foreigner and *porteñas* definitely don't want to. Back home [in my small European country] I dance all night."

It certainly can happen that a man is a great dancer and, nevertheless, finds it difficult to get any good dances here in Baires. This might be because he goes to milongas with an exceptionally high proportion of young professionals (such as El Yeite), difficult territories to break into. Or to milongas where he is a lot older than average (an older foreign man might be an excellent dancer, but it is less likely to be the case – so people may be less likely to take a chance on him). Maybe he is unpractised at using cabeceo. Or maybe his visit is very short: it can take a little while for the women to recognise a desirable partner. Or it might be just sheer bad luck. I can certainly think of cases in which good dancers were unjustly overlooked. But, whatever the reason, some visiting men take this very much to heart, especially if, in their home communities, there is a surplus of women and they are unused to ever sitting out a tanda involuntarily.

But many many men have come here and spent night after night in a hundred different blissful embraces. I've heard a lot more happy stories than complaints. And they came from almost all corners of the globe, with skin colours ranging from 80% cocoa to skimmed milk and some look as Chinese as Confucius or as Swedish as Bjorn from *Abba*.

Many women in Buenos Aires love to dance and don't get to dance as much as they would like. I hear all the time, from my Argentine table neighbours at *El Beso*, "that Hindu [sic] over there with the funny beard thingy, can he dance?" "have you danced with that little Korean guy, can he dance?" Some people do have convoluted motivations for choosing dance partners. But most of us women are searching for something much simpler: pleasure. I couldn't care less whether my partner is a third generation *tanguero* who was born and bred in La Boca or if he just warped in from the planet Endor and has pink antennae sprouting from his forehead. If he is blissful to dance with, bring it on.

On the difficulty of getting dances with new people

It can be extraordinarily difficult to get to dance with a new person who is a classy dancer: even if they have seen you out on the floor with excellent dancers; or dancing socially with their teachers; even if you consider yourself one of their peers (rightly or wrongly);

and even when good dancers are few and far between and you think you might have some scarcity value. Most good dancers are choosy and risk averse, eye contact with them is elusive: they play hard to get. Catching their attention, being considered a possible candidate for a *tanda* and maybe finally getting to dance with them can be a process of glacial slowness.

Although I don't fully understand why many of the good dancers are so reluctant to dance with new people at their level – that is simply how it is. I just wait out the long slow process, hoping that, gradually, person by person, I will win at least a few of the choosy ones over. I'm working on them, as in the *Cabaret* song, *inch by inch, mile by mile, step by step. Man by man.*

Setting your heart on a specific partner or partners

If you set your heart on dancing with a specific person at a major tango event, you risk severe disappointment. If they are as immune to your strongest laser *mirada* as if they had been wearing special safety goggles, you can quickly feel like the singer in *Rondando tu esquina*: "I can think about nothing but him at the start of every new *tanda*/This consuming passion is terrible!/And he doesn't even know, doesn't even suspect/My desire to dance with him."

On the other hand, when the stars are aligned and you find yourself in the arms of one of your favourite dancers – that one who has the ability to make you feel not that *he* is a great dancer, but that *you* are one – just as your favourite orchestra is playing, then you should torch your oldest, loosest pair of heels and make a burnt offering to the tango gods, play a Di Sarli in their honour and offer up an hour of solo walking per day.

It's always tempting to lament the *tandas* you didn't dance, to brood on the rejections: "but, but, but… I really wanted to dance with *him* and *him*." And to forget the experiences of bliss, effortlessness, playfulness and deep immersion in the music. My tango marathon was rich with beautiful *tandas*. And, as for those who did elude the powers of my *mirada*: watch out. I'll be back.

Why I don't dance with certain leaders

First of all, I look at the embrace. Is he (or she) holding the follower awkwardly off to one side or tucked under his right armpit, like a man carrying an unwieldy golfing umbrella just in case on a sunny day? Is he holding his partner in an unnecessarily open embrace? That often signals a very raw beginner. I also notice the leader's right hand: is it pulling her clothing askew, moving around a lot, paddling or rubbing at his partner as if she (or he) were a computer mouse or are his fingers clawing into her? I reject a lot of leaders based on the sight of them gripping their followers' backs. If you're doing *anything* with your right hand except resting it lightly, I probably won't want to dance with you.

Then I look at the follower's face. I usually interpret scrunched-up faces or rolled eyes as an extreme measure, a sisterly warning, like a buoy in front of dangerous rocks. *Beware.* Don't sail here or you will be shipwrecked.

Does he try to step inside or outside the follower by awkwardly thrusting his hips forward? Is he doing any stagey moves, such as lunges, dips or huge *volcadas* and *colgadas*? Does he rush ahead with his moves and then wait for the follower to catch up? Is he blocky when he turns? Is he unable to create space for a forward *ocho* towards the closed side of the embrace, leader's right? That's a sure sign of not being able to separate out different parts of his body and of moving with a certain robotic quality.

Does he look uncomfortable in his own skin? Trembly or wobbly? Is he lunging his way through a gazillion rock steps (I prefer to save lunges for the gym)? Is his head thrust forward into the follower's space? Does he walk like an Egyptian? I know from experience that having someone else's head in my space makes for a VERY sore neck. Is he slaloming around the floor willy-nilly, like an Uber driver in a hurry? Do his eyes dart around in a panicky way? Or does he look spaced out?

There are a few social indicators, too. I will say an automatic no to someone who walks up to ask me to dance at a formal milonga where that is clearly discouraged or prohibited. Anyone who marches up to me with outstretched hand, is arrogant in any way, or otherwise seems as though they would be astounded by a refusal also gets an automatic "no, thanks." What that says is either "I have never been to a milonga before and have no clue what's going on" or "I can't imagine why anyone else would choose one partner over another."

There are people who feel nicer to dance with than they look. And there are a few people who look nice but feel stiff. With borderline cases, I will give them a whirl (if they're willing) to see what they feel like.

But there *are* things that can be seen from outside, which almost never feel good. I'm not talking about aesthetics here, but whether the person looks *comfy*. And, preferably, with some spark of creativity, some *je ne sais quoi*, hard to define but easy to recognise. It's not enough for the person's dance to be just *not awful* – it has to have positive appeal, too. Some things never feel good: careering around the floor, being stomped on, being gripped in the mid back, having to bend your neck at a weird angle, being made to step off the music, etc. You don't always need to try someone out to know that you wouldn't enjoy dancing with them. Especially if you have a trained eye.

Why I don't dance with some really lovely people

Let's assume I encounter a leader who is doing everything right to the best of his ability. His (or her) floorcraft is impeccable: I know we will be safe from collisions. He's not attempting any fancy moves he hasn't mastered. He's not going to squeeze, crush, push or manhandle me. He smells of a freshly-ironed shirt, soapy-clean male skin and my favourite perfume. And he is a truly wonderful human being.

I still might not choose to dance with him. Why not? Because doing things simply in a way that is pleasurable for the follower is not that easy. It's not just a question of good intentions, of being a kind, gentle or empathetic person or exercising common sense. It's a lot subtler than that.

I sometimes liken an unsatisfactory dance to a long conversation over instant messaging with someone who replies "LOL" to 90% of your messages. It can give you an ego boost, but it can feel empty, too. They aren't giving back. Sometimes, such dances feel like talking to someone who you know is lively, intelligent and fun – but who does not speak your language, with whom you can communicate only in pidgin and gestures, just when you are longing for a sophisticated conversation.

In tango, the things you need to give back include dissociation (which sounds simple but is *not* intuitive). That twisty sensation is an intrinsic part of the feel of the dance and once you're used to it, without it, everything can feel tasteless, bland and robotic. You'll also need musicality (which requires technique to express with subtlety); groundedness, a sense of really owning the space; and a gentle but committed embrace (which also requires technique – you can only embrace the other person well if you yourself are balanced, flexible and moving smoothly).

However good your intentions, you cannot give someone something you don't yourself have. There's an African saying: *never trust a bare-chested man trying to sell you a T-shirt.* It's not a question of intrinsic human qualities, intellectual knowledge, or the right attitude – you also need physical skills for which you will need to train your body. We almost all overestimate the extent to which we possess those skills.

So what can you do? Learn to love dancing with those who happily dance with you. Work on your own skills in the hope of giving and receiving more pleasure on the dance floor, as time and money permit. Focus on increasing your own resources, on what you have to give to partners.

And, meanwhile, there are few things more blissful than dancing with your peers. The sensation of giving and receiving equally is the highest joy our dance has to offer.

What makes me more likely to dance with someone?

Here are my criteria for choosing.

If I haven't had a chance to observe the person out on the floor, then I will be influenced by their posture in normal life and how they are dressed (appropriately for the venue is better). But the single most important factor will be *how* they ask me – a method of selection I call '*cabeceo* triage.' If an unknown man asks me to dance verbally, I'll almost certainly say "no, thanks." But I may well respond positively to a *cabeceo*.

If I *do* get to see the person dancing, it's easy to choose. I can spot the better dancers in a room almost immediately. They stand out like bright red poppies amid a field of grass. Even if I can only see their heads, I can often identify them by the smooth quality of their motion. Their dance may have rising and falling elements or dramatic changes of dynamic, but it will lack an uneven, jerky quality or a vague, meandering, directionless feel. The good couples are smooth waves amid a jagged landscape, rolling hills amid the crevices and crags.

I'll be looking for clean footwork, a seamless flow to individual movements, judicious use of pauses and spiralling torso action. I look for leaders who are accompanying their followers' movements. I'll avoid anyone I catch standing awkwardly hunched over waiting while he tries to get his partner to do things. I look for an embrace which looks comfortable. In marginal cases, I also examine the follower's face – a fixed frown or darting eyes are the milonga equivalent of a one star Trustpilot review.

I don't have to tick all these items off some mental checklist. These are the things I spot almost immediately, without even trying.

How can I tell whether I'll enjoy dancing with someone?

I can usually tell what people will feel like to dance with because I have a "trained eye." Let me explain how I have trained that ability.

It's mostly unconscious practice. I've sat at milongas, watching specific people dance, and then, afterwards, have danced with those same people – so I have a direct comparison. I'm a *lot* better at telling what leaders will feel like than followers, since I mostly dance with them and am therefore used to calibrating the precise correlation between look and feel. But I also teach part-time and watch students to try to spot problems with their dance and I frequently dance with them and video it and then try to show them on the video what I am experiencing – deliberately searching for the visual expressions of things that I am feeling in my body.

I often find that you can feel something is off, but you're not quite sure what it is – until you look at the video, when you spot the problem instantly.

The Slow Semite and I video ourselves every practice session. It provides us with a bright yellow post-it note of what needs to be worked on. Sometimes it reveals a fault of which I was blissfully unaware – difficult to detect and isolate from within the embrace, but glaringly obvious on camera.

There *are* things that cannot easily be seen. One is the degree of pressure with which someone is touching. I can see whether a leader is holding his (or her) follower way off to one side, can spot fingers which are obviously clawing or tugging or an embrace which looks frozen and rigid. But I cannot tell whether the follower is touching her (or his) partner lightly or clutching at them and clinging on for dear life by *where* she has placed her hand or whether her fingers are open or closed. And, while a raised left elbow on a leader *looks* awkward and tense, I've danced with enough left-elbow-raised boys who felt smoother than butter to know that some people's arms are perfectly relaxed in that position. The amount of pressure you exert on the other person is important in tango and it's something you can't always tell just by looking. Sometimes dancers are stiffer or softer than you were expecting – but softness versus tension is only one aspect of what makes a good dancer.

The other thing which is hard to detect is the degree of musicality. The tiny slowings-down and speedings-up, the somatic *rubato* of our dance, the teeny changes in response to shifts in musical mood or to a partner's suggestions – I can usually get a sense from watching of whether that degree of sensitivity, of reactivity, is there within a dancer or not. But when I dance with them I often feel more of it than I was expecting from watching. This may be partly a placebo effect. But some people, by altering things by almost imperceptible fractions, give me the feeling that they are exceptionally musical. That isn't easy to see.

Tango is an integrated system. It's not like ice skating. I'm not awarding points in my head for different aspects of the dance: 6 for dissociation; 8 for musicality; 4 for embrace, etc. The better dancers all dissociate smoothly, embrace comfortably and express the music sensitively: you can't improve very much without improving all aspects of the dance. Generally, those better dancers can be spotted instantly, often without even seeing their feet – there is a general underlying cleanness and clarity: like radio stations sounding amid the static as you turn the knob, like swans gliding smoothly amid a flock of bobbing ducks.

I can't always tell how good someone will feel. There are times when I think "hmm, I wonder if I would enjoy dancing with him or not." Then I'll shoot a *mirada* in that direction and try him out. But I'm not that often in doubt – because I have a good sense of what I'm looking for.

Different people feel good to us at different stages of our own dance

Many leaders feel wonderful to less experienced followers because they scoop them up and carry them, compensating for their poor balance by holding them upright in firm embraces, muscling them through movements which they are not responsive enough to follow smoothly without the use of a little additional force. It's a bit like standing on your dad's feet at an age when you can barely toddle alone, while he walks around, carrying you with him like a tiny marionette. More experienced and skilled followers may avoid those leaders, however, since being treated like a puppet doesn't feel good once you are used to moving independently.

Many leaders feel disconcerting to less experienced followers because they lead fast movements, which require reaction speeds that take years of training. Or very slow movements, which are deliciously luxuriant, but require balance and control. Or simply because they don't help; they don't offer a Zimmer frame, they don't hold you up or guide you through each movement.

Many followers feel wonderful to less experienced leaders because they allow themselves to be pushed, pulled and manipulated through a wide range of movements. They are willing to throw their heads back campily and go down into that stagey backbend, immune to embarrassment. They know that that odd combination of pushing with the right arm and pulling with the left is your signal for a forward *ocho* and will obediently go there.

Many followers feel disconcerting to less experienced leaders because they will not respond to a confusing signal. They won't cross when what is being led is not the lead for a cross, even though they can hazard an educated guess that, in the leader's mind, a cross is intended. They respond to what is actually happening somatically, not to what the leader might be thinking. They stubbornly refuse to be pushed or prodded and stand rooted to the spot if you attempt to shift them by brute force. They will not do those ankle-deep bone-clashing *ganchos* you learned last week in class and step away in dismay when you try to pull them into a vertiginous *volcada*.

The dance is created jointly. There is a limit to how much you can compensate for each other's failings. And there is a very serious limit to how well you can judge someone's dancing, or how rich an experience of their dancing you can obtain, if you cannot fulfil your own part.

The 'sometimes' partner

Many of us have two kinds of people we are happy to dance with: *Sometimes Partners* and *Always Partners*.

Perhaps – especially if your community is a small, intimate one – there are people you want to dance from time to time because they are nice people or to keep up local morale. You may not get that much dance pleasure from them but it feels good to make them happy, on a human level.

But there are times when you really don't want to dance with the *Sometimes Partners*: when your favourite orchestra is playing; a very desirable dancer is about to ask you; your favourite partner's favourite orchestra is sounding and you know they will invite you to dance it with them; the *ronda* is chaotic; you are about to dance a goodbye *tanda* with a dear friend you won't see for a while (who is an *Always*); or you are weary in mind or body and don't have the mental energy to create a good dance with them.

This is one of the reasons why it's important to allow everyone to choose not only *who* they dance with but *when* they dance with them. Always assume that you may be some people's *Sometimes Partner*. Even if *they* are *Always Partners* for *you*. Accept that, while nothing feels as delicious as being each other's *Always Partners*, being a *Sometimes* can be nice too. Life's too short to turn your nose up at it. Being a *Sometimes* is a lot better than being a *Never*.

Groucho Marx syndrome

Groucho Marx once famously quipped: "I wouldn't want to be a member of any club that would have me as a member." Some people wouldn't want to dance with anyone who would want to dance with them. I call this *The Groucho Marx Syndrome*.

Why do less skilful dancers so often feel such deep resentment when more skilful dancers decline to dance with them? This isn't always a question of not getting to dance at all. In most scenes, less skilled dancers outnumber the more skilled. In fact, one of the problems of becoming more skilled, as *Tango Cynic* points out in the video *The Loneliness of the Long-Distance Tanguera*, is that you tend to enjoy dancing with a smaller number of people. So, if you are less skilled and many other people around you are also less skilled, those other unskilled people are your comfort zone, your pool of potential partners, your crewmates and comrades-in-the-dance. "What are you resentful about?" someone might ask, "You have lots of partners!" You need to simply find the milongas where those people go. Find your tango tribe.

Part of the answer is this: many people are unable to enjoy dancing with those at their own level. This sometimes stems from a discomfort with their own dancing – they need a partner who is able to compensate for their problems. And sometimes from an overly-sensitive awareness of the imperfections of their partners, a constant, irritating consciousness of all the mistakes intrinsic to dancing at a less advanced level.

Groucho Marxism is a common ailment in tango, a side effect of the fact that our dance is technically challenging in its early stages. But once you shake off the Groucho Marx syndrome, the wormhole will open, your shuttle will hit maximum warp and you won't care whether *The Enrosque Emperor cabeceos* you. Because you'll be too busy exploring the galaxy.

Why are we so selective about partners in tango?

Perhaps it is partly to do with the embrace, with its sheer physical proximity. And perhaps partly to do with what we cannot help hoping for, as we put our arms around someone to dance: a playful romp through the music together; a sensual, melty, dreamy loveliness; a lively duet; a chance to express ourselves; a wish to luxuriate in the delicious twistiness of *ochos* and the silky smooth glide of walking.

As soon as I feel I am just going through the motions – whether it's because I feel repeatedly manhandled in ways which my body intuitively resists; or rushed or made to step off the music; or feel a frustrating tension just where I would like to ease in and snuggle – time seems to crawl to a sluggish pace as if those twelve minutes will never be over. Even with partners who others may love dancing with, who are delightful human beings or whom I enjoy hugging off the *pista*.

But especially with those who have little self-awareness when it comes to their dance. There is a complacency which leaves me feeling: "Did you really want to dance with *me*, specifically with me?" A lack of curiosity – whether because of a smug assumption *or* an anxiety about their own dancing which doesn't leave them enough peace of mind to explore the partnership between us – a sense that they aren't interested in discovering what *my* dance has to offer is the most deadening thing. So, sadly, those I am most likely to decline to dance with are probably least likely to understand why.

I am blessed in having wide-ranging tastes in partners. But I'm also cursed in not being able to enjoy everyone. Against my own best interests in many cases and at the expense of causing upset in some situations and becoming unpopular in others, I find that bringing myself to dance with someone I don't want to dance with is one of the hardest things to do.

The question you should never ask

There are two kinds of questions that it's not a good idea to ask: ones that are likely to elicit the response (spoken or silent) "none of your business!" and those that you may not *want* to hear an honest answer to. "Why won't you dance with me?" is an example of both.

It's extremely difficult to frame this question in a way that doesn't sound accusatory. And when people do answer, they seldom answer honestly or provide information that you could act upon.

The reason may be personal – they simply don't like your vibe. The reason may be something you cannot change (age, body type, attractiveness) or something completely unrelated to you.

You might think you have nothing to lose by asking, but, actually, there have been people who have danced with me often, stopped for a long time and then begun dancing with me regularly again. I'm very happy indeed that I didn't try to call them out on their reasons for not dancing with me at the time.

They may be rejecting your dancing, not you

When someone declines to dance with you, please bear in mind that what they are rejecting is very often not you, the person, but your *dancing*. If you are working on your dancing, your dance will change, develop and hopefully improve. That's why a rejection usually means "not now, maybe later" and is not just a yes or no valid for all time. There are many people I used not to enjoy dancing with who are now favourite partners of mine. And vice versa.

Different levels of fussiness

I have two friends at opposite ends of the scale of choosiness and I often find it useful to channel one or the other. When I'm dying to dance with some buttery smooth leader whose eyes turn glazed and blank whenever they meet my longing *mirada* gazes, when my bottom is numb from an unlucky evening of involuntary sedentariness amid a crowd of beautiful dancers locked in melty-looking embraces from which I am excluded, I channel my friend *Foxy* at her absolute fussiest. What would *Foxy* say? I think. "Why do you want to dance with that guy anyway? He's got great technique but there's no real musicality or feeling there. He's just a *salony* clone." And that guy? "He's OK, but are you sure you really don't mind the way he squeezes your fingers with his left hand when he leads *ochos*?" "Those guys are none of them as good as they *think* they are." I think: would he meet *Foxy*'s standards? If not, I'll calm my envy and play the game of seeing-things-through-fussy-eyes.

But the person I channel most is *Miss Marple*, whenever I wish I could enjoy someone's dance more. I know she would say "well, yes, he's a little overly forceful when he leads those *giros*, but he's so in the music," "yes, he does have a tendency to tug you there, but I love the way he slows down for those violin passages in the Troilo."

Countless times, channelling *Miss Marple* has allowed me to get past minor technical irritants, quiet the inner voice that says "I wish he would stop doing that" and find pleasure in leaders I might have otherwise dismissed. And, countless times, channelling *Foxy* has helped to cushion my disappointed ego on a low night.

So find your *Foxy*, find your *Miss Marple*. Channel them when you need to. You can't change your own personal level of fussiness. But you can sometimes make some very useful little tweaks.

Future investments

I sometimes hear beginner men say that when they become good dancers they will 'take revenge' on the women who decline to dance with them now. I have never actually encountered a real-life case where such revenge was extracted: probably because men with that attitude almost never become good dancers. And I've also heard the reverse: that you should dance with promising guys *now* as an investment, to 'train them up,' *Ecole des Femmes* or *La Nouvelle Héloise* style, to be a fit partner for you in future. Sadly, this rarely works either. If the guy is dedicated and ambitious enough to become as good as or better than you are, he will probably progress to other partners. Which is why if I dance with a beginner leader at the milonga, I do it because there are aspects of his dance I enjoy, *right now*. Not because of hopes or fears for the future.

Rediscovering old partners

Many people have noted that it's possible to grow out of your enjoyment of a particular dancer, especially if you liked to dance with them as a beginner but, now, despite your best efforts, cannot take pleasure in their dance any longer.

But there is a flip side to this. Once you're well past beginner stage, when you get to dance with an old favourite partner again, after a period of months or years, you can almost always revive the spark. It's not about a search for perfection. You can be keenly aware that they are not dissociating enough *here*, that their right arm is tense *there*, that they tend to rush those *giros*. But all that is outweighed by the sheer accumulation of beautiful moments: of all those sensations of diving together into the music and retrieving glistening pearls of sound made motion – clumsily clutching at them sometimes; at other times scooping them up graceful as a dolphin; but always retrieving and bringing them to light. The dance is a remembering at the same time as it is an experiencing: each movement is both satisfying in itself and brings with it memories of *tandas* danced in other cities, other hemispheres, and other periods of your life.

It's like finding an old forgotten dress in your wardrobe, trying it on and feeling "aha! it still fits; it still suits me; it still feels comfortable against my skin."

Missing specific partners

People often say to me "how can you miss dancing with *Snugglebunny* when you have so many great partners in Buenos Aires?" But each dance relationship is unique. Each partner has their own delicious charms, their tender way of holding you, playful interpretation of the music, signature moves and quality of deeply attentive, concentrated listening: to the music and to you. Long after I've forgotten most of the detail of what happened on the floor, I'm left with a hormonal, neurological memory. As the saying goes, I will never forget how they made me feel.

I've flown across continents chasing an embrace: in one case, not even knowing if he would be there at the milongas, heart thumping as if waiting for a date, nervously scanning the room in search of a familiar pair of twinkly brown eyes beneath a thatch of unruly hair. Tango is profoundly polyamorous: my loves are multiple. So, no, I don't miss *Snugglebunny*. I long for him; I crave him; I ache for him. And, yet, I have no desire for romance, no wish for sex, no prospect of anything more – or less – than a beautiful *tanda*. But I can feel the tug of that from halfway around the world. I am waiting for the powerful magnet which is Buenos Aires to lure him back to the shabby charm of our southern city, to the polished circle of wood in the upstairs room with the long green curtains concealing the traffic of Corrientes beyond, to *Cachirulo*, to my *mirada*, to my arms.

The people we wish we enjoyed dancing with

Many of us have people in our lives we heartily *wish* we loved dancing with. They are kind, sweet, sincere, favourite drinking buddies, loyal friends. Wrapping my arms around them in real life gives me the warm fuzzies. And yet they feel so tense, blocky, wobbly or robotic in the embrace. Loving someone's dance is no more something I can control than falling in love with them. I can no more make myself like it − against all my strongest inclinations, ignoring the pull of the music and the instincts of the body − than I can make myself want to French kiss someone. Even if I would love to give them the experience of how I feel when blissed out in someone's tango embrace − I cannot.

But I watch those people closely. I wait patiently. I check in with their embrace from time to time. I nurture a quiet hope that they will transform themselves in time into people I love to dance with. Few things feel as wonderful to me as when my affection for the person and my joy in their dancing merge. When the person begins to fully inhabit their body, move with confidence, feel and respond to the emotional tug of the music and begin to own it − when they start to feel delicious to me − that, my friends, is one of the best feelings in the world.

Limits to our freedom of partner choice

I am a fierce defender of freedom of dance partner choice. I believe no one is ever owed a dance nor should anyone ever demand a *tanda* as the price of their friendship or love. Protecting your own body from harm and unwanted proximity is a deep-rooted instinct (we always choose, welcoming certain kinds of physical closeness and avoiding others).

But there are a few situations so extreme they give me pause. There is the case of the professional tango couple who performed and taught together but who never, in the course of three years, danced a single *tanda* with each other at the milonga because, as the girlfriend told me, "he doesn't like dancing with me." There are the guys invited to a private wedding milonga who refused to dance a *tanda* with the bride because "she isn't a very good dancer." There is the guest teacher who spent several months living with a host couple and danced not one single *tanda* with the wife, over the course of dozens of milongas they visited together, sharing a table and drinking his hosts' champagne. (These are male examples, by chance, but actually this is not a sex-specific issue, although it can be easier for men to avoid unwanted dances than women).

There was a very minor situation I was involved in not so recently. An acquaintance came to find me at an informal milonga, sat down next to me and engaged me in conversation. I talked for a while, feeling a little guilty impatience as I was in the grips of an especially strong longing to dance. "You know," he said, "one of the things I've learned from my visits to Buenos Aires is that the milonga isn't about dancing. It's mainly about meeting friends and chatting. It's really nice to be able to spend time hanging out without dancing. It's much more relaxing." "*Hmm*," I said, "that can be true. But I usually really want to dance. Tonight, for instance..."

The conversation continued to flow and meander for another couple of *tandas* and I tried with all my might to focus on our small talk and not seem too impatient to be freed up to look for dances. Until a very lovely Di Sarli-Podestá *tanda* began to play. "Ahhh!," he said. "This music *really* makes me want to dance. Doesn't it you?" He looked at me meaningfully. "Yes!" I said, hopefully, making the first movements towards getting up from my chair. But then he unmistakably looked past me and his eyes scanned the room and caught someone else's and he gave them a discreet nod. "Nice talking to you," he said. "But NOW I am off to dance!" I can't get past the memory of that incident, insignificant as it was. I have nothing to reproach him with. But the awkwardness sticks with me.

Tango people, especially the better dancers, are often accused of unfriendliness. But these kinds of sticky situations remind us that combining dancing and socialising is a difficult balancing act. Sometimes, it really is better to separate and compartmentalise. To share a table in a restaurant but go your separate ways at the milonga. Don't attend the wedding if you really cannot bring yourself to dance with the bride.

And sometimes you might not enjoy the *tanda* itself, but you will feel like a better person for dancing it. I *do* regret some *tandas* I didn't dance, with people who would never have dreamed of pressurising me, but who I sense would have been delighted to have had those dances. I wish I were now looking back with pleasure at *having given those dances to them*.

Occam's razor for your stubble

There are so many people opining loudly online that people in their local scene don't dance with them because those people are "members of cliques." Or because they have a strict table of people's 'levels' as dancers and they (the complainants) have been allocated to the wrong part. Or even that third parties have told people not to dance with them because that would make them look 'uncool.'

But, in all the cases I am personally familiar with, those complained about are the better local dancers and those they "exclude" by not asking them to dance happen to be the dancers whose dancing is less developed. Coincidence? I think not...

Use Occam's razor, folks. If people you would enjoy dancing with decline to dance with you, there could be many reasons. They could have sworn an oath sealed with their own blood to never dance with someone who wears your glasses prescription or has a freckle on their left shoulder. Or perhaps they don't dance with you because they know or suspect the dancing would not be a pleasant experience for them. Which seems more likely to you?

The 'babe/bitch' effect

A friend used to wear a T-shirt that said *Babe* on the front and *Bitch* on the back. The message was clear: the pretty girl approaching, smiling at you is a babe. The same girl retreating, ignoring your overtures, is a bitch.

I think we've all felt it: that guy over there with the beautiful *enrosques* and *lápices*, the one who strides so confidently through the music, whose partners all wear an expression of deep bliss – he seems like an elitist wanker, a cold and aloof person because he won't invite us to dance. And, then, suddenly, *joy of joys!* he looks over and gives us the cock-headed signal of *cabeceo* and we are out on the floor with him and *ah!* he is wonderful. He is soft, musical, sensitive. And suddenly we're convinced that he is actually a warm and lovely person. We were *so* wrong about him.

My friends, beware of this effect. Don't judge someone harshly just because he or she declines to dance with you.

Would you really prefer to be rejected for yourself or for your dancing?

I often hear people voicing the reassurance: don't worry, if people aren't dancing with you, it probably has nothing whatsoever to do with whether or not you are a good dancer. It surprises me that people are comforted by the idea that their rejection might be based on personal rather than dance factors. If people don't want to dance with me because they don't know me, I can change that, gradually. If they don't want to dance with me because my level of dance is too low, I can change that too, through lessons and practice. But if it's personal, that's far harder to change.

Dance rejections can hurt, but rejections of who I am as a person? *Ouch.*

Personal relationships between tangueros can be very awkward

On the one hand, we hold each other in our arms and participate in intense experiences of mutual bliss. It's almost impossible not to feel a fondness for someone with whom you experience that kind of pleasure: subtlety of communication, sensuality and the witty flirtatiousness of shared musical jokes. It can be disappointing sometimes when they are awkward around you off the floor: it's like waking up to a silent, hurried breakfast and a bleary-eyed, mascara-smeared walk of shame after a passionate one night stand.

Towards those we don't wish to dance with, there can be another kind of awkwardness, a shifty sort of compromise between being friendly and not giving them false hopes that you might dance with them, especially if you are in a situation of enforced close proximity in which a direct refusal would be clear, visible and therefore especially guilt-inducing. It feels rather like being on a blind supper date with someone who is leaning in towards your chair, beaming with happiness, as you try to strike a balance between kindness and coldness, having already decided in your mind that you find them impossibly physically unattractive and cringing inwardly with the guilty fear that they might attempt to snatch a kiss.

This can make sharing tables at the milonga a social minefield. It can be wonderful to sit with your peeps and be surrounded by a bevy of lovely *tangueros* who you know you will get many blissful dances with over the course of the evening. But it's not always like that. As a beginner, I often had the experience of being part of a table of people who greeted me with cheek kisses and back slaps and then ignored me for the whole evening, clinking champagne glasses over my head, turning their gazes blank or suddenly assuming manic, fake smiles if I looked in their direction, in order to avoid the meaningful kind of eye contact which all too clearly expresses a desire to dance.

Conversations with members of your own role can be oddly stilted too, broken, hesitant, as both parties keep one eye out, scanning the room, hoping to catch the glances of invitation, like someone having a conversation with you while watching television out of the corner of their eye. (At home, growing up, conversations were generally conducted to the drone of a TV accompaniment – I hated it).

Sometimes tango relationships can feel forced, strained or even icy off-piste because of their undefined nature: we exchange lover-like gestures on the floor, yet sometimes we're barely nodding acquaintances in real life. We share a public space, but would we really choose each other's company freely otherwise? Are we friends or just virtual strangers who happen to be at the same milonga? The boundaries are fluid and that can lead to feelings of ambivalence and confusion. Nothing makes people more socially awkward than that.

My favourite dancers are my peers

Most of my favourite partners of all are not top-level world-famous dancers. Most of the most memorable *tandas* I've had have been with people I consider my peers.

The top level dancers, it's true, can take you deeper and further into some aspects of the dance. You can feel the movement in its platonically ideal form, frictionless, perfectly balanced, grounded, smooth as ghee, free from the most minimal tension. You can be challenged by more rapid changes of speed and direction than you've felt before, forced to bring your speediest responses. It's a valuable experience which gives you a lively awareness of the exciting possibilities of our dance, a sense of how far there is still to go.

But, while I love the dance as an art form, I love it more for something else: diving deep deep into the music with someone who is as interested in my dance as I am in his (or hers), someone capable of being excited by my ape-shit urges in D'Arienzo, someone who luxuriates in my languor in the late Di Sarlis or wants to share my passion in the Puglieses.

Someone who is also interested in *me* – not necessarily sexually or even as a friend. But someone who wants to experience *me as a dancer* in a twelve-minute marriage of imperfect equals. Those are the best *tandas*, for me. Not the ones of highest technical expertise.

I find Justin Trudeau as sexy as the next woman (perhaps more). But it's the boy next door who I will actually crush on.

Psychological Factors

The importance of play

Practice is fundamentally about conforming: taking your body's unconsidered motions and honing them to make them more like the kind of tango you wish to dance. There is a platonic ideal somewhere in my mind, a perfect walk, a flawless *ocho*, and I want to edit away all superfluous gestures, file down and smooth off all excrescences, remove all eccentricities and oddnesses which detract from what I am trying to express, rid myself of clumsier movements. But there is always a risk that this process of stripping down, of "cleaning up," as my teachers always put it, is a form of impoverishment. That babies will be flushed down the drain with that murky bathwater. That, as everything that is not elegant, that doesn't feel smooth and effortless, is pruned away, you may suck away the flavour with it, the intuitiveness of your responses to the music, the expressive idiosyncrasies of your personal dance.

That's when you need to slick on your lipstick, sling your shoe bag over your shoulder and head for the milonga. To forget about your aspirations to be pretty and instead just *be*. To let your head bob and your knee bend too much, your foot slip and your steps be stompy. To focus on using every movement and gesture at your disposal to express the music in the full palette of colours, even the muddy ones, drawing with every pencil, whether blunt or neatly sharpened. That's the way to find your own dance, the contribution you can make to the partnership in play. You need to forget about yourself, your quest for self-improvement, with its demanding self-scrutiny and self-monitoring and give yourself over, lose yourself in the game. There's no time to analyse your backhand: the ball is heading your way. You can't lose sight of it for an instant.

Self-consciousness

Being in the arms of a good partner and feeling confident about your dance is one of the best feelings in the world. And feeling self-conscious or insecure is one of the worst.

One unfortunate side effect of practising a lot is that it increases your self-consciousness triggers. You can get very accustomed to the sensation of thinking "yes! this time I really nailed it" and immediately afterwards hearing "tell me – why is it so hard to feel your weight changes? why does it feel as though your hips are up in the air like that?" or "[insert your own current technical concern here]." But if you want to progress you need to be able to switch the self-criticism on and off at will. For class and practice, set systems to niggling, pedantic self-awareness. For the milonga, banish that inner critic, dive into the music, hug and play. It can be easier said than done.

I discovered this afresh last night, when dancing with *The Leprechaun*, the most delicate, dainty, tiny, swift-footed, petite little person at the entire milonga, Ariel fluttering around his small, oval island of polished wood and crimson columns, a magic elf scattering fairy dust in his path.

I began with a feeling of "dammit; I am going to make him enjoy this; I am going to seduce him into submission with the gorgeous sensuality of my dance continued on to "right, fine, it's fine; I feel powerful and confident" – which I used as a reassuring mantra – and ended, with a whimper at "I'm sure right now he is painfully conscious of all the things that are wrong with my dancing and is grateful for the mercies of the *cortina*." And, although this was my first time dancing with *The Leprechaun*, I've danced with my own teachers socially many times before – and even performed with one or two of them (a *far* more high-stress situation).

In dance, you have to switch from poet to proof-reader, from reveller to policeman, from blushing lover to stern chaperone. And back. Again and again. No wonder there are occasional hiccups during the handover of powers from pedant to playmate.

Recovering lost confidence

Dear *Terpsi*,

My confidence took a real bashing recently after some critical comments, sighs and tuts from a tanguero I'll call *Mr Hotshot*. I was in tears in the ladies afterwards convincing myself that I was totally deluded about my abilities and everyone else who had danced with me was just being charitable, polite, etc. etc. I've not really got my confidence back since.

What do you think is the best course of action? I'm thinking of getting some intensive private lessons. But I don't want a complete deconstruction back to absolute basics because that will just finish me off for good. I want to get past where I am now, in a sort of scared limbo land. That phrase 'you can't give love until you feel it for yourself' – well this is how I feel about my tango now – until I have faith in my own abilities, I'm not going to give 'good tango' to anyone else.

I've started to dread and avoid going out! I know that sounds pathetic coming from a woman many would describe as 'strong, independent, confident' – well not in tango!!

Abrazos,
Lost Confidence

Dear *Lost Confidence*,

First of all, I am disgusted by *Mr Hotshot*'s behaviour and I appeal to everyone, especially women, not to tolerate partners who teach you on the dance floor, much less those who tut, roll their eyes or are in any way rude. If someone behaves like that, break *tanda* – no matter how much of a big famous fancy pants he is.

So, how do you recover your confidence? Seek out those milongas where you have had good experiences in the past. If you can, contact your friends and favourite dance partners and ask them if they are going. Knowing that you will encounter people who love dancing with you will help a lot.

Taking private lessons with rigorous teachers who focus on the fundamentals of your dance and doing solo technique practice will help to build your confidence in the longer term, but I agree that that might not be the best strategy right now. You need to take the focus off yourself. Tango learning has two parts: the serious half is technique. But then there is the music, which is sheer enjoyment and play. So I would focus on listening and learning, dancing solo and trying to find new ways to interpret the music, adding decorations, varying tempi, finding ways to make your leaders hear what you hear, finding your personal voice as a dancer. You'll never be technically perfect – but you can always offer your specific character as a dancer and that has to do with how you hear the music and interpret it in your own movements, both in *adornos* and in general quality of movement and micro-adjustments of timing.

All dancers go through phases in which they lack confidence. Never apologise for your dancing. There will always be some people who don't enjoy dancing with you. But there will be others who will. Seek them out. They are out there!

Abrazos,

Terpsi xxx

Tanda anxiety

At some milongas, I am like a kid standing on the pavement outside a sweetshop, my nose leaving grease prints on the display window glass, salivating at the display of liquorice shoelaces, stripy candy canes, snowy marshmallows and crinkle-wrapped, beetle-bright mint humbugs. I want to reach my sticky fingers into those jars! That is the first element of *tanda* anxiety: simple desire.

Then, beyond that longing for blissful experiences, the junkie's ache for the needle, there are complicated questions of status anxiety. I confess: I want to be recognised as one of the serious dancers. I want to play with the cool kids. I want to be seen out there on the floor, demonstrating that I can twist and whirl through rapid changes of direction, that I can express my love for the music by picking up the details with rapid, flicky free feet. I want to show both my partner and others that I can dance, I'm worthy, I'm fun, I'm snuggly, I can swim and I don't need armbands or a rubber ring. That I can go out of my depth, leave the kiddie pool and get into lane with the serious swimmers.

Then there is the paranoia which can rear its ugly head. Why are those who usually dance with me avoiding my gaze tonight? Is it something I said? Something I did? A rumour that is circulating? *Mr Elegant Enrosques* and *Mr Whirly Giros* always used to dance with me, but it's been ages since our last *tandas*. Have they stopped for a reason? Oh, God, is this a tendency? Are all my favourite partners going to desert me?

It may not be listed in the DSM, but *Tanda Anxiety* is definitely a mental illness. Those of us already lucky enough to have experienced many wonderful *tandas* have to try to find inner calm, stop trying to up the ante, increase the dose and chase that fierier dragon. In the very wise words of a friend "only in Buenos Aires could you have an evening of lovely *tandas* and still feel disappointed that you didn't have even lovelier ones." If you can identify with this, you are not alone. We need a support group, my friends. I don't always feel *Tanda* Anxiety, of course. But sometimes it hits me pretty hard.

Don't measure your self-worth in tandas

Comparing notes with my friend *The Biagi Lover* one morning, I discovered that we danced the same number of *tandas* the night before – around half a dozen each, and all of them very lovely in my case. So why did my friend feel happy with her experience while I seemed to descend slowly but inexorably into a morass of self-pity?

Well, one factor is that, much as I love *mirada/cabeceo*, it can be unsettling in some situations. When you have or had a close emotional connection with someone in real life and they are repeatedly meeting your eyes with glassy, blank looks at the milonga, it can feel like a rejection of more than a *tanda*. We can forget the conventions of the dance for a moment and find ourselves regressing to the instinctive sadness we would feel in normal life if a friend wouldn't meet our gaze or looked unresponsively through us. We have only the language of eyes to communicate with: an idiom which is subtle, opaque and prone to misunderstandings.

Then, there is no denying that how often you dance can be a gauge of your attractiveness as a dancer – and, perhaps, as a woman, too. It can feel like a giant real-life game of "Hot or Not?" It's a lek and we females are displaying our feathers. Popularity contests and attractiveness competitions are always stressful – unless you are sure of winning.

My friends, don't measure your self-worth, sexual attractiveness or even just your skill as a dancer in number of *tandas*. Just treasure and cherish every set you *do* dance, every single lovely song.

Otherwise, you will leave the milonga as I did that night, feeling like a reject and a failure at love, tango and life. Your head may get stuck very deep inside your posterior, as mine did. It is dark and smelly in there and there's no light at the end of that damp tunnel.

Musical pedantry

I am quite baffled when people tell me things like "I love these Di Sarlis with Podestá but I can only enjoy them when the DJ also plays Caló and Fresedo earlier in the evening"; "I can't enjoy this beautiful *tanda* of D'Arienzo-Maurés because the DJ played instrumental De Angelis twenty minutes ago"; "I can only like these Canaros with Famá under certain very specific circumstances"; "I only like to dance if the DJ has played the orchestras I like, in the order I prefer to hear them, for the whole evening."

I've never understood this idea that tangos are time-dependent. That *Fuimos* loses all its beauty if you play *Desvelo* beforehand. That you can no longer take pleasure in the beautiful violin and bandoneon solos at the end of Troilo's *La Maleva* if the DJ played a vocal as the previous track. That we can never hear or dance to certain gorgeous tracks because the orchestra didn't record four songs that same year with the same singer and therefore those numbers can never be played within a *tanda*.

For some, a *tanda* they didn't enjoy seems to leave a burning taste in the throat, like a pickled onion, making it impossible to enjoy the chocolaty richness that might follow. A song they disliked is like a mint thrown into their glass of Coca Cola.

It's useful to arrange tracks in *tandas* that make sense so that dancers know what to expect and can choose partners accordingly. It's not a good idea to put a very obscure song first because many will not dance to it and will lose the entire *tanda* as a result (in crowded places, *mirada/cabeceo* can become impossible after the first song). I support good craftsmanship when it comes to *tanda* construction.

But each *tanda* is its own microcosm, each song is its own world. They aren't enjoyable only in the context of a perfectly ordered musical universe. What's important about a tango song is not the exact year it was recorded, but the moment, now, in this current year, that you are dancing to it. *Carpe noctem*, my friends, pluck the night's flowers one by one! Don't let pedantry about the arrangement of the full musical bouquet spoil your evening.

Why I care what people think

"Who cares what people think? Be yourself and let them worry about how to deal with it." That's excellent advice in many areas of life. But, at the milonga, I care what the good dancers think. I care if they are looking askance at me because I'm leading a *tanda* or two. I care if I am dancing with someone who makes me look clumsy out on the floor at a time when I know people are watching. I care that they will think I am too over-eager, too 'desperate' if I eye them too much. I care that I can be socially awkward and that my attempts at deadpan humour sometimes go down like a beaker of cold sick. I care that I may look unappealingly chubby in that dress or wrinkly without my concealer. I care that people may disapprove of what I write.

I care for a very simple reason. I *really* want to dance with the good dancers. I care what they think if it will affect whether or not they dance with me.

Sometimes I feel that same anxiety I had when I was back at school, where few of the other kids would be my friends. But, as a child, the cool kids who weren't my friends didn't have anything to offer me. The things I enjoyed doing – reading and taking long walks – I enjoyed doing alone. Whereas now I really want those cool kids/good dancers to like me – because I want them to dance with me. So the milonga sometimes makes me feel like a child again – and not in a good way.

The three Murphy's Laws of the milonga

At the milonga, there is no correlation between how much you want to dance and how much you get to dance. In fact, a Buenos Aires milonga is an excellent place to resoundingly disprove the magical thinking that if you only desire something strongly enough you can somehow 'attract that energy' and 'make the universe' give it to you.

Instead, some much more banal laws are in operation.

The first law of the milonga is that the more desirable and attractive an unknown dance partner looks, the more difficult it is likely to be to get dances with them. The consequence of this is that the more desirable unknown people there are at a milonga, the fewer dances you will get there.

The second law is that there is almost no one you can depend upon to always dance with you. If you are thinking "at least X is here, he *always cabeceos* me" – it's precisely on that night that X will avoid your eye.

The third law is that, whenever the conditions of the first and second laws apply, you will also have a seat with a semi-obstructed view and would require a wing mirror to be able to perform certain angles of *mirada*.

Fall foul of the first, second and third laws and you will dance few *tandas* that night.

Serendipities

A night at *Cachirulo* always makes me aware of the serendipity involved in finding dance partners. A lot is dependent on your seat and sightlines: there are almost always some people you can't dance with because you cannot see them well enough – or they cannot see you. In addition, a favourite or regular partner may be dancing few *tandas* that night and, after attempting to catch your eye once or twice, give up – while you were, meanwhile, quite oblivious to his glances, letting your own gaze stray across the opposite end of the room, unsuccessfully seeking dances there.

Glances can miss their mark all the time. Mistakes are made and after discovering once or twice that the look and gesture weren't directed at you but at your neighbour you can grow disheartened and write that person off as a potential partner. You can look longingly in someone's direction just as they've decided to take a break for that *tanda* or have caught another elusive partner's eye. You can give up on someone clearly looking in another direction or wait to see if they are unsuccessful in their ocular wooing and turn to you instead. You can miscalculate or not notice the eyebeams shot at the back of your head. Even two people who want to dance with each other, might not dance that night, for a whole variety of reasons.

But while that means that nothing is guaranteed, it makes it all the more surprising how often our ocular flirtations are reciprocated. And it makes it all the sweeter when those magical *tandas* happen.

The Abrazos Scale

The Abrazos scale is a rather like the Richter scale, an exponential scale for measuring tango bliss. It runs from 1 (so unbearable you cannot finish the *tanda* under any circumstances) to 10. If you actually experience 10 Abrazos, you will be struck by such intense bliss that you will go into instant cardiac arrest and drop down dead right there on the dance floor.

I often find myself talking about dancers' "skill levels" or about whether a particular milonga has "a lot of good dancers" or not. While this can be a useful shorthand, it's probably more fruitful to think in terms of personal tango happiness. And that means finding the milongas and partners who give you high readings on the Abrazos scale. We almost all have them – it's often just a matter of locating them.

Running with the fast crowd

If there's one single difference between dancing at home in Buenos Aires and in the diaspora (particularly in the US), it's this: at the milongas I go to back home, I am always in the company of at least a few dancers – and, on a *really* good night, many – who are better than me. More physically skilled, more responsive, more elegant. Teachers, role models, YouTube idols – pace setters.

In some ways, I am more comfortable in the diaspora, among so many of my fellow Salieris, without those Brylcreemed, fake-eyelashed virtuosos to demonstrate silently, with every step "who are you trying to kid? this is how it's done!" Some of the nursery slopes of the diaspora can be very gentle on a humble climber's ego. On these alpine meadows, just pop an edelweiss behind your ear, and you can feel like an intrepid mountaineer.

In Buenos Aires, on the other hand, you are constantly being confronted by dancers who seriously outclass you. That's challenging in both good and bad ways. It's always a little difficult to stomach the idea that someone else may be better than you at something you

107

have a deep passion for. Even if you know that their entire life story has been different from yours and every choice they have made has led them to this: from their first duck-footed steps in ballet class at the age of six to their murderous daily marathon practice regimens on four hours sleep, eight gourdfuls of *mate* and half a pack of cigarettes.

Here the meadows are far away: we are up in the mountains. The air is thinner and people can feel you panting. Time to train up your lung capacity, even though you will probably never reach the summit. It doesn't matter: this is not a race. And let's be grateful for the Sherpas who set the pace.

Dancing in a new place

People – including me on occasions in the past – can be very quick to judge a tango scene inaccessible or 'snobby' after only a single visit, even though generalising from a sample size of one never yields reliable data.

In his book *The Quest for the Embrace*, Gustavo Benzecry Sabá writes that, in the Golden Age, new single visitors to a local social club's milonga often had to spend a month just sitting and observing, before they were accepted by the locals enough to be invited to dance. So, surely, we moderns can hold out for a night or two?

When you are in a new place, you usually need to factor in at least one frustrating night trapped in the classic catch-22: if no one has seen you dancing, no one will ask you and, if they don't ask you, they won't see you dancing. The catch-22 is usually broken eventually, but not necessarily on the first night. No one is to blame – and, beyond staying good humoured, there is little that can be done. Just know that, like the measles, it's something that has happened to most of us. And from which we can usually recover.

Strategies for enjoying a milonga even if you're not dancing

The first thing I do if I'm not getting dances is get a glass of wine and resolve to treat the milonga as a wine bar-concert, enjoying the music as intensely as I can and viewing it as an opportunity for listening practice, for learning that music by heart, listening out for new nuances, etc. Listening to good tango music is never wasted time. (If I dislike the music, I usually just call it quits and go home).

Then, I watch the dancing intently. If there are technically good dancers out there, I try to learn from them.

Then, if the geography of the room and circumstances make it possible, I try to make friends with the other women and find someone fun to chat to – though I try to resist chatting during the first song of the *tanda*, to avoid interfering with our chances of receiving a *cabeceo*.

And, finally, I enjoy singing along to the tangos (including the instrumentals). When the Malerba *tanda* comes on, I almost prefer singing along to it than dancing (I find Malerba very singable).

Despite these tactics, I do get frustrated sometimes if I can't get dances and occasionally get a little grumpy in those situations. The ideal is to get plenty of great dances. But being able to enjoy a milonga at which you sit a lot is an important skill to have.

Performance

Roses and champagne

At *El Beso* one night I watched my favourite tango couple, Carlitos & Noelia, give one of their most beautiful performances. In a rose pink dress and champagne-coloured shoes which blended with her skin tone and made her look almost nude, the focus was very much on her luscious body in very graceful motion. They were both less rough-edged than usual, her toes were more pointed, her movements tighter and cleaner. He wore black, like a stage hand, silently and unobtrusively placing the flats, positioning the scenery, creating the backdrop. Having seen her dance socially with a number of different fellow-professionals, I was especially struck by the special qualities of their partnership, the way that he, with his energetic but simple, never flamboyant dance, sets up frames which she fills with musical decoration and play, hints and suggestions which she takes and runs with, as they choose, together, which parts of the music to emphasise, which details to linger deliciously over. He is like the ideal pianist, accompanying the singer with unobtrusive virtuosity, making every note sound richer and fuller.

Everyone I spoke to mentioned the performance, including people whose own style of movement and embrace is very different from theirs. Everyone talked about the way they expressed the music. They seemed to embody and bring to life all the feelings I had about those songs. It was like having read a favourite novel and stepping into the cinema to find that the director's casting was perfect, that the actress he chose for the lead role was someone I would never have thought of but who, as soon as she appeared on screen, convinced me: that's *exactly* how I imagined her.

People often complain about the ill effects of performances, that watching dancers perform flashy, acrobatic moves will encourage beginner dancers to attempt steps they haven't mastered and create chaos in the *ronda* with their flailing *boleos*, clumsy *ganchos* and unpredictable lungings. Performances have an influence on how people dance if they are moved by them. But that influence can be a very beneficial one, too.

You can feel as if a little of the couple's spirit had taken possession of you, making your own body more scrumptiously sensual and imbued with musicality, more elegant and precise in motion. As if it were no longer you, but a vehicle, a sleek and shiny sports car with the top down on a mountain road, a horse you climbed upon to gallop through the meadows. Those aren't your legs – bulky and clumsy and mottled with the mosquito bites of February – they are a pair of magical paintbrushes and the floor is your canvas; together with the music, you are a poem already written, a perfect sonnet, and all you have to do is read it aloud in a confident voice.

The Biagi Lover and I, sitting out a rare *tanda* together, watched the floor swirling and striding joyously to the Laurenz instrumentals and agreed that that was some of the most musically rich and expressive dancing we have yet seen on a social floor. I think the performance had a little to do with it. It was an inspiration.

Two contrasting couples
At La Baldosa with Los Totis and Carlitos & Noelia

All my favourite couples have a distinctive, unmistakable style, their own signature look, embrace, musicality, quality of movement (and probably also technique – though great technique is frequently invisible, like the cement foundations buried underground, the veins and arteries beneath the skin). My favourite couples have all found

110

the way of dancing that frees them to express everything they need to, that feels right to them and that fills them with sheer tango joy. When you look completely at ease in a certain style, it no longer matters to me which style it is.

One night at *La Baldosa* we had two couples giving performances, and you would be hard pressed to find more contrasting pairs. First, Los Totis: a pair of lithe, elegant dancers, stretched tall, upright and proud, his feet whisking through a dizzying number of beautiful leader decorations, crossing and uncrossing and *boleo*-ing amazingly deftly, flicking carelessly perfect *ganchos* between her legs as she circled him a dozen times in succession, the silky skirts of her backless gown floating on the air. Not one step went unadorned from either party, not a toe was unpointed, every moment was distinct, precise and balletic. And then Carlitos and Noelia: two chubby little Munchkins (by comparison), her generous curves poured into a leopard print dress, bottom wobbling a little in the fast movements of milonga, pouncing on every movement with a rushed suddenness just this side of ungainly as he almost stomped his way around the floor. It was gritty, rough-edged and sexy. I loved them both. *Vive la différence.*

Solo Tango Orchestra

How wonderful it felt to be immersed in their music. To feel the double bass deep in my tummy. To watch and hear the impassive-faced bandoneonist (as serious as a master comedian telling the most hilarious of jokes straight-faced, as earnest and unmoving as a champion poker player) coax such a variety of plangent sounds from his instrument; to hear the pianist, hunched Nosferatu-like over his keys, alternate between channelling Rachmaninov and bar room honky-tonk; and the violinist playing my favourite instrument with such sweetness, such a variety of different tones and timbres.

And all of them playing arrangements which were close to the classic, familiar ones, but yet subtly different, so that we were forced to sharpen our ears to hear the changes – and every one of them sounded brilliantly right – and playing those arrangements with such subtly compelling *rubato*, stretching here and compressing there.

They played with an intoxicating combination of precision and feeling. The phrasing was clear and yet not academic: they put body, heart and soul into it. Their guest singer, Sergio Ugarte, was a molasses-rich but clear baritone. Dancing to them was thrilling, too, as I discovered when *Pretty Salony Boy* rescued me with a *cabeceo* just as I was about to fling my knickers at the violinist.

I'm not usually a huge fan of modern tango bands. But these guys got a well-deserved standing ovation from my usually fussy and blasé fellow *porteños*. Those Russian boys totally ROCKED the house. *Спасибо*, Solo Tango Orquesta. Now that's musicianship in the service of tango.

How it feels to perform with a nervous partner

If you've never done a tango performance before, a few things about the experience might surprise you. First, no matter how relaxed you *think* you are, you may feel your jitters setting in in response to the cues of your name being mispronounced through a crackly microphone, all the house lights being turned up to their full blaze, stepping out onto a floor you are used to sharing with a hundred other couples to find it eerily vast, a huge expanse of glimmering wood, as daunting as a pristine blank screen to a reluctant writer, and catch glimpses of what can seem like row upon row of expectant faces.

And then your partner's body is a surprise, too (if he or she gets nervous). Their skin can have an unfamiliar tangy scent, the scent of fear (even if they normally smell only of perfume and freshly-laundered shirts) and there can be an unmistakable shaky trembling just where you are used to relying on rock-solid stability. This can range from a very slight fluttery sensation in their upper body where it touches yours, through a sweaty right hand that slips constantly out of your grip or shakes like a flag atop a weather station on an especially windy day, to a full-blown blancmange-like wibbling and wobbling all over, making you feel that you are trying to dance around a maypole made of butter. These are conditions which no amount of practice could prepare you for, since they will only happen on the night. However it measures on the Richter scale – faint tremor or complete avalanche – performing can feel like dancing in the midst of a minor earthquake: though some of the seismic activity, if you're lucky, may subside after the first few bars of the song.

When this happens I try to provide an extra dose of Zen, to be extra grounded, extra calm, extra precise. Not to dither, but to make clear, unequivocal gestures. To make my decorations not the desperate doodles of someone trying to force ink out of a dried-up biro, but the brush strokes of a priest, painting a temple scroll with glossy black ink.

Performing is a useful exercise. It forces you to develop the clarity and confidence you should always have in your dance, under especially difficult conditions. It's combat training, a stress test for both of you. Though it definitely gets easier each time. And, afterwards, social dancing feels as effortless as dreaming.

The joys of performance

I love the intimacies of social dancing and, when following, I am rarely conscious of anyone else besides my partner. My eyes are closed in close embrace, or fixed on the man's chest at nipple level in open. The only times I am really aware of other people are during the rude awakenings of minor collisions. But I believe I dance my best when I *know* people are watching – especially dancers I admire and friends I love.

I remember dancing in a little group performance one night. As I traversed the giant ballroom in a state of intense concentration, as I flicked, whirled, tapped and lifted my free foot furiously, trying to catch every syncopated nuance of the D'Arienzo, I had an enveloping sensation of being part of something larger: both of that group of wonderful dancers (like a dream mini-milonga) and the huge festival we were part of. A couple of times, I even caught someone's eye among the spectators. At the far side of the hall, I made accidental eye contact with a woman at one of the front tables just as my partner paused and left me to decorate a double-time passage in milonga with a free leg whisking like an egg-whip and, instead of looking away, I sustained her gaze, grinning cheekily. "Look! this is fun" I told her with pointed foot and twinkly eyes.

Usually tango is a discreet, though often eavesdropped-upon, *tête-à-tête*. But performance is about communication with a larger group and to be heard you need to make your movements bigger and more visible and, above all, clearer and more definite. Being clear about what part of the music you wish to express, exactly *how* you want to move and the movement quality you are choosing, being precise in your signals, eliminating fuzz, noise and vagueness, having the courage to do what you want without confusing hesitations and dithering: those are crucial skills for any dancer and performance can foster them.

And performance makes you want to give your all. If you are a baroque painter like me, it makes you want to snatch at every single detail, letting nothing escape the swishy, swirly, stipply brush of your free leg, painting ephemeral lightning sketches on the air, recording your feelings about your partner and the music, capturing them and then letting them dissolve, like a child chasing rainbow-shimmery soap bubbles.

The reason my heart thumped so hard was not just because I was dancing with an exceptionally energetic partner who loves to lead fast movements and changes of direction (musical whirlwind Dan Boccia) but also because I felt "folks, this is it, this is as much as I can give you right now, this is everything I can get out of these songs. I wish it were more – I'm going to bust this curvaceous arse of mine to make it more – but this is everything I've got right now and I've put it here into my body in motion."

Dancing should always be like that. And performing can give you a taste of it.

Floorcraft

How Free is the Free Leg? Following and Floorcraft
Responsibilities

After a terrible accident at a San Diego milonga in which a woman's ankle was severely gouged, I thought long about the extent to which followers can be held responsible for collisions on the dance floor.

If the follower is decorating, i.e. adding an unled movement to express the music, then clearly she (or he) bears responsibility for anyone she might injure. This is one reason why I prefer smaller, subtler *adornos* over larger, flashier ones. Large, high decorations performed blindly with the follower's back leg, including *boleo*-like *adornos*, are inadvisable for obvious reasons.

But, with led-and-followed movements, things become far murkier. Some followers add extra energy or impetus to a lead, turning what should have been a small, gentle movement into something unexpectedly huge and violent. Occasionally, leaders even expect this (when the music is very punchy, for example).

But to what extent is the follower able to control, change or tone down something that has actually been led? This is difficult to define. Most of us followers have had the experience of dancing with a beginner leader and standing rooted to the spot as he attempts to *volcada*, *colgada* and *boleo* us as ineffectually as if trying to move a stone statue. (I once spent an entire *tanda* fighting a valiant battle against a beginner determined to make me do tibia-clashing, ankle-level ganchos. And I ended the *tanda* with my ankle *gancho* virginity intact.) But, at the other end of the scale, most of us have also experienced magician leaders who, with seeming effortlessness, make us do things we didn't even know we were capable of, harnessing the laws of physics and making them do their bidding, changing direction at the precise moment required to make our free foot arc out around us in a wide circle or fly through the air before we even realise that anyone has led a *sacada* or high *boleo*.

As followers, we train ourselves to develop intuitive, incorporated responses to leads. We need to read what the leader is suggesting as accurately as possible and react quickly and fluidly. Following begins

115

with feeling an impulse and responding. I feel the leader preparing to step forward and I find myself preparing to step back. There's no moment at which I think "OK, do I trust this guy? Should I take a back step?" And yet I cannot see behind me and I don't know if the space I am stepping back into is unoccupied or if I am about to crash into an innocent fellow dancer. But still, calmly and confidently, my body responds to the signal and I move backwards around the *ronda*, safe and happy in my partner's arms, even though I am not looking where I am going (in fact, I frequently close my eyes). The same is true, to a greater or lesser extent, of all led-and-followed movements. There is potential danger, but, in general, I trust the leader to navigate around any hazards.

Is it possible to modulate those responses according to conditions on the floor? To sometimes let the leg fly freely and sometimes keep it tightly controlled? To a large extent, yes. We followers need to stay aware of navigational difficulties – to be sensitive, even with closed eyes, to additional tension in the leader's body, a sense of physical urgency which signals "tricky traffic conditions ahead." But sometimes a highly skilled but perhaps not so floor-aware or considerate leader will make my leg fly before I know it, at a very unfortunate moment. Far from this being me 'showing off,' I am embarrassed and generally hope no one noticed. Could it have been prevented? Perhaps. But I personally was unable to prevent it. I am not surprised by that. We followers aren't trained in resistance. We are trained in responsiveness. The sensation of the *boleo* itself is like seeds being blown off a dandelion clock. It's not force, but delicate lightness applied with impeccable timing which seems to fill my leg with helium.

If you see a high *boleo* happening at a packed milonga and find yourself muttering about the irresponsible follower who did that *boleo*, then remember this: for many of us, *boleos* aren't something we *do*, they are something that *happens to us*. Followers have different thresholds as to when their feet will fly high. If you want to avoid your partner's leg from lifting in *boleos*: learn to lead low ones, clearly and unequivocally, so that *every* follower will respond with a foot on the floor not in the air. Or leave them out of your movement vocabulary when you're at a very crowded gig.

But remember this, next time you see one happening. The follower probably isn't thinking "*shazam!* take that and that, you imbeciles! watch my lethally-sharp stilettos slice the air and keep your distance!" She's probably thinking: "Oops! How did that happen?"

I'm not convinced that any follower who causes an injury to another should be summarily condemned, hung, drawn and quartered. Or her partner, for that matter. We all need to be more aware of those around us in the milonga. Leaders, especially, need to work on their floorcraft skills and followers also need to exercise some discretion and awareness. This is a question of knowing and respecting the conventions of the *ronda*, of mastering improvisation and being able to change direction speedily if necessary, not leading flashy moves when there is no room for them, developing good spatial awareness, valuing quality of movement over quantity of moves, having good technique to provide us with balance and control so we are not as likely to fall heavily or to employ excess force and treating the limitations imposed by other people as spurs to creativity, not just hindrances. All these things are learned skills. Beginner dancers may not yet have them – which does not make them bad people. These are technical, not ethical, questions. It's not just about keeping our *boleos* low.

Quite honestly, I do not know a single veteran dancer who has *never* been involved in a collision on the *pista*. Or has never been at least partially responsible for an accident. Rather than focusing all our energy on heaping vitriol onto the wearer of the stiletto concerned, let's look to ourselves first.

Following when it's crowded and chaotic

It's certainly challenging for leaders to dance at *De Querusa*. That long, humid, echoey cave quickly fills up with high energy, creative young dancers, not all of them highly skilled or very experienced. But those kinds of spaces are difficult for followers, too. Even for followers who dance with closed eyes in close embrace and follow leads intuitively. Since, even if you aren't actively trying to *help* the leader navigate (a practice about which there are different schools of thought, but which I personally avoid), you'll need to hone some very specific skills.

In particular, you need to be able to sense when your partner is doing emergency steering, having to abort a particular movement or to change direction rapidly and in a counterintuitive way, to avoid a collision. As a follower, you have to stay absolutely and utterly alert in that situation and it presents difficulties of balance at times too – such as pushing off for a long step, almost arriving and then, *swoosh*, no, not quite, let's rethink that, which is exactly the kind of situation that can make the most grounded dancer wobble.

But what's most crucial is heightened awareness of the leader's level of urgency. This is hard to describe, but easy to feel. It's not necessarily about speed, it's about a cutting off of things halfway through and a sense of "OK, I know I was planning an *ocho* there, but just trust me, leave it unfinished, come with me over here instead."

Following on a crowded, chaotic floor takes skill too. As so often in tango, we have different roles, but it's still teamwork.

On those who complain about the lack of 'progress' in the ronda

I love the tango walk, parallel system, in close embrace, as much as any dancer could. But *giros* and other circular movements are just as much a part of our dance as the lovely determination that characterises our gotanian perambulations. Pauses, both long and short, are some of our dance's most delectable moments.

Everyone who fetishizes 'progress' in the *ronda*, please consider this: it's not a race, it's not a road that takes you from A to B. You're still dancing when you use circular and non-travelling movements. For reasons that I expect a physicist could best explain, all populated *rondas* tend to become *giro*-heavy, rather than walking-heavy, spaces, no matter how ardently people proselytise the pleasures of pedestrianism. But that doesn't make our dance any less delicious.

And as for 'getting somewhere,' well – how can I break this to you gently? It's a circle. You were never going anywhere in the first place.

Complaining on the dance floor

It must be very annoying when other leaders have poor floorcraft. It is only human to occasionally let off steam and make a

118

remark about this to your follower. But some leaders seem to want to share every detail of their frustrations with the floorcraft of others. Mostly, when I hear something like "God that guy in front of us was so annoying!" or "When is he going to stop dancing that interminable *giro* and walk?" I have had my eyes closed, in close embrace, with my back to the direction of dance and have absolutely no idea what my partner is talking about. But, even when I do know, there is not much I can do about the way other leaders are dancing.

I like to think of a *tanda* as a little like a mini date. Constant complaining doesn't add to the quality of the experience. I have been on dates with men who were very complimentary about me, but found fault with absolutely everything else. I didn't go on a second date with those guys. In the case of the leaders, I will dance with them again if they are good dancers. But we would probably both enjoy ourselves more without the litany of criticism.

The Leader Train

One of my favourite phenomena is what I call The Leader Train. The first couple of hours of a special milonga can be a little chaotic and frustrating. Leaders cut into the *ronda* unexpectedly, overtaking "in lane 1.5" or weaving around unpredictably. But after a while, the magic starts. Our partners enter the *ronda* at the invitation of a quick, complicit exchange of eye contact, a discreet nod from the leader behind them, holding position for a moment to allow us to take our places and wrap our arms into an embrace. It always gives me a miniature frisson of pleasure when that happens. Leader *cabeceo* is a classy thing.

And then, when we stop between songs, we can look around and see all the leaders strung out in a line, equidistant from each other, as if each couple were a thick black point in a child's join-the-dots drawing. They have formed The Leader Train.

The *ronda* is our enchanted chalk circle, the canvas on which we paint. And the more stress-free the navigation, the more we can focus on the music, our partners and the dance. One of the things I most love about tango is that it is a social dance. We dance together, sharing a space. Let's avoid a tragedy of the commons; let's respect our shared environment. Be the kind of leader good dancers would enjoy having in their train.

Crazy dancing at Malcolm

I don't know many dancers who enjoy crowded floors and almost everyone is stressed by not-quite-as-crowded-but-extremely-chaotic *pistas*, especially those filled with expert (or not so expert) dancers dancing their huge, energetic, fast-moving, highly improvised and therefore unpredictable dance. *Villa Malcolm* can be one of the most difficult of floors when it fills with high-powered young dancers, whirling through *giros* in every conceivable direction, follower free feet bisecting the air in *boleos*, pouncing on every rapid passage of the music with catlike alternations between sudden dramatic stillness and explosive bursts of speed.

One couple at *El Motivo* is the floor space equivalent of five at *Cachirulo*. I wouldn't advise a beginner leader to get out onto that floor under crowded conditions unless you are the kind of person who doesn't mind riding your bicycle on the fast lane of the motorway.

I don't think I've ever danced there without hearing at least a dozen confessions of man-on-man homicidal desires, a few incredulous bursts of laughter ("really? seriously? you're going to go *there?!*"). While I rarely collide with people myself, this is because the leaders tend to act as shock absorbers.

Since I have only ever once been privy to a physical altercation between two leaders who didn't appreciate each other's floorcraft skills, I actually think social relations at *El Motivo* are a testament to the young men's anger management skills. Collisions are acknowledged with a brief nod or eye contact or ignored altogether. There's rarely any drama.

But, while no leader seems to actively enjoy this aspect of the dance, it does have some beneficial effects. You are forced to improvise. In the process you often discover new possibilities. You have no time to think: you have to let your body respond and find the movement that you need right there and then. As *The Slow Semite* put it: "cool stuff just happened and I don't know what it was." It's the nearest you get, as a leader, to following, i.e. to understanding what it means to move in response to someone else's signals.

Dancing at *Malcolm* can be hazardous. But it is also creative, exciting and alive. I doubt that kind of dance – so full of improvisation and exploration – could ever have developed if everyone danced alone in practice rooms. Other couples aren't just obstacles: they are a constantly shifting framework that shapes our movement, provides restrictions that stimulate creativity and adds an element of serendipity to the leader's role. So try not to hate other people on the floor any more than you would hate a tennis opponent who made you race from one side of the court to the other. Challenges can really up your game.

Beginners at Milonga 10

Perhaps it's not your fault. Perhaps the more experienced dancers *ought* to be more considerate and give you more space and time, as you're a beginner. Perhaps they *ought* not to lead such huge, loopy, kick-your-own-arse *boleos* in crowded conditions.

But there are certain floors – and *Milonga 10* at peak hours is one – where the floorcraft is difficult. The dancers are very experienced and, while there are often minor collisions and sudden avoidance manoeuvres, there are almost never major incidents causing injury because those experienced dancers have quick responses, a wide vocabulary of moves and directions of movement and can turn on a dime, change a back *ocho* quickly into a forward one, do whatever is necessary to avoid injury.

If you're a beginner leader and have slower responses and can't change direction in response to someone coming towards you at speed, if you find that when you have a collision it's always pretty serious because you fall onto your steps or bang against the other person suddenly and unexpectedly, *Milonga 10* at peak hours, with Biagi or D'Arienzo playing, is probably not the right environment for you. If you were a learner driver would you go straight out onto the freeway on your first day behind the wheel? I hope not.

I don't like to dance with beginners (whether temporary or long-term) at crowded places with lots of people dancing high energy big moves. In those circumstances, I feel like a human crash test dummy. I cannot relax and enjoy the *tanda* knowing that there is a high possibility of being spiked by a stiletto heel.

Leaders, please note: keeping your follower safe is a priority. If you think she is likely to get injured dancing with you, that's a problem, no matter whose 'fault' it is. And that means that sometimes you just have to stay off the floor.

The Wedding Dance

I am often surprised by how decently most people dance under two circumstances: when the dance floor is very small *and* when people have had a few glasses of wine (both circumstances are necessary, in combination). When the space available is clearly limited and people know they have been making multiple champagne toasts and that their balance is probably not at its optimum, they often have a better sense of their own limitations.

Instead of attempting to yank the follower into some strange back *sacada* with *gancho* combination, it suddenly seems more prudent to lead a simple *ocho cortado*. Careering around the floor in an open embrace doesn't seem as attractive a proposition, suddenly, and people start holding each other in close embrace.

There is no shortcut to learning many of the skills which will make you a lovely person to dance with. You can dance small and modestly and still be not dissociating, have a stiff left arm, be out of the time with the music, etc. But most really bad dancing at the milonga is the result of leaders punching above their own weight, trying to force steps they haven't yet come anywhere close to mastering or of people holding their bodies stiffly away from each other and trying to do moves at that distance.

Under the circumstances of a tango wedding (tipsiness and spatial constraints), the worst excesses disappear. The social dancing looked pretty and felt snuggly. I wish I could capture that feeling, bottle it, and spray it liberally around at normal milongas.

Floorcraft as a reason for declining to dance

Deficient floorcraft is perhaps the least often mentioned of the reasons why we might choose to decline to dance with someone. It's true that many of us will happily leap up and fold ourselves into the arms of a leader whose dance is creative, but who has his (or her) fellow *ronda* travellers swearing under their breath or tensing up (I can tell immediately when *Pretty Salony Boy* is impatient with someone he considers a road hog from a tell-tale twitch in his left arm; *The Slow Semite* tends to squeeze my hand). But there certainly *are* circumstances in which it is the most salient factor.

122

It's the only sensible justification I've ever heard for the fact that, in places where verbal invitations are the norm, men tend to ask women to dance and not vice versa. It's the guy (or leader) who needs to handle the floor conditions – and not be tempted by an offer from a desirable partner to launch into a *ronda* in which he would not be able to keep her (or him) safe.

There are definitely leaders with whom I will not dance if conditions are crowded, hectic or fast-paced, even though I would enjoy dancing with them in a different environment. This is especially true for women leaders, among whom I include myself. We often simply have less *pista* experience than our male counterparts. This is a self-perpetuating cycle from which it can be difficult to break free: we're not used to navigating in crowded spaces, so we avoid leading at those milongas and thus never build up the requisite floor time. This is the one aspect of our dance which can really *only* be learned at the milonga. But it's best to take the learning process slowly, always erring on the side of caution.

Also, swervers, backsteppers and dangerous drivers of both sexes, please be aware that other leaders may hate you and make their opinion known to *their* favourite partners. There are certainly guys I would love to dance with, were we to encounter each other in the middle of the Gobi desert, but I look steadfastly away from them at my crowded local tango joints – because my favourite partners are driven almost to distraction when they have to share the floor with them. I don't want to be part of that and risk becoming the innocent object of other dancers' wrath or even angering favourite partners so much they stop inviting me themselves.

Before you neglect your floorcraft skills, remember this: it's a social dance. If you dance antisocially, there may be penalties.

The challenges of an exceptionally crowded milonga

Some nights, *Cachirulo* reaches saturation point. If any more dancers were to appear, some of us would have to vanish into thin air. I remember nights like that. It can get a little chaotic: I swish my bottom with unintentional sexiness back and forth against a leader's buttocks; my hip catches painfully against the edge of a table, making bottles rattle dangerously; another follower's stiletto grazes my ankle.

Locals like to blame collisions on visiting Europeans and Americans, used to their thinly sprinkled milongas, their wide-open barn-like venues. But they are not the only culprits. At this density, it becomes difficult to fit each couple's dance into the *ronda*. It starts to feel like a rather complex jigsaw puzzle. But I love to see the place full of tangueros, bursting with a mixture of the old and young, professional and amateur, local and visiting.

If you've never experienced a very crowded milonga, when you do you'll begin to understand a few things about tango culture which may have seemed mysterious before. Such as why we don't block the floor between *tandas*; why people often dance only one *tanda* per partner per evening (there are so many favourite dancers on our wish lists); why even the *saloniest* dancers tend to spend 80-90% of their time in close embrace; why *mirada/cabeceo* is the fastest and most efficient way to get dances (if you had to fight your way through the crowds to get to your desired invitee every time you would never make it onto the dance floor, whereas a mimed transaction takes seconds); why people don't usually get quite as precious about floor craft violations or rigid about rules (you can't or your blood pressure would soar so much you'd have an aneurysm); why followers are often reluctant to dance with inexperienced leaders – it's really scary to be out on that floor with a reckless or overly-timid driver, you've got to have confidence in your pilot; why the milonga has such an intimate, social feel to it; why so many excellent leaders have never done a *colgada* in their lives; and followers do so many teeny tiny subtle little decorations (perhaps you would too, if you spent the evening dancing ten thousand *ocho cortados* in succession – wholesome fare, yes, but more delicious when jazzed up with subtly different spice mixtures and condiments each time).

Partnering

My friend: So, you are a close embrace slut. And I am a close embrace gigolo.

...actually, I'm not a real gigolo because I don't get paid. I'm a *pro bono* close embrace gigolo.

* * *

Richard Slade's T-shirt design for leaders: on the back, in small letters "If you can read this, you're too close." And, on the front, "If you can read this, you're not close enough."

* * *

You are somewhere, at the milonga, and you invite a woman to dance [by *cabeceo*], and in that infinitesimal space of time which passes between getting up from your chair and going to fetch her: how long is it? fifteen seconds? ... after fifteen seconds you are embracing a woman who is a stranger to you. The possibility of intimate communion which the embrace offers is the secret of tango. (Javier Rodriguez, my translation)

* * *

"Ultimately it comes down to what you want in a dance, is it an exploration of technique, musicality and conversation with another person? Or is it to make friends and have fun? Listen to the music and the lyrics; though it can be, for me, tango is not about fun, it's a whole experience that is more akin to making art, rich in shades of grey." (Mike McCarrell)

* * *

"When I leave here, I might get run over by a bus. But at least we will have danced this beautiful Donato *tanda* with each other."

* * *

Embraces

The embrace is a miracle

I am often surprised that most of us take such a wide range of people into our arms. We catch the eye of a stranger, across the room, signal willingness with a brief mime, stand up, wrap an arm around his (or her) shoulders, nestle our heads against his neck, hold his hand as trustingly as a child, close our eyes and let him encircle us in the warmest of hugs, with not the slightest reluctance and not a trace of worry, fear or reticence. There's no moment at which we negotiate – *this close and no further* – or decide on an optimum distance. We go straight to the closest we can be, while still in a mode of absolute gentleness.

It's not so astonishing, surely, that we are not willing to do this with everyone at random, that we watch, observe and choose first. It's not so surprising that we are particularly eager to hold those dear to us. What's surprising is just how warmly we embrace complete unknowns. What's startling is that the embrace is possible with so many people: dozens over the course of an evening.

No matter how often *The Slow Semite* and I work on the minutiae of our posture and hand positions in the embrace, it's never just a dance hold to me. It always retains the quality of a real hug. There is always that moment of first contact, as the *tanda* begins, when we know we're not on the planet Vulcan anymore, signalled variously by a beard soft against my cheek; a cushioned belly that I rest against happily, like a waterbed; a delicate thinness that I wrap myself around; the firm contours and familiar hardness of a muscular chest; long strands of hair escaping from a ponytail or man bun tickling my ear; the top of my head velcroed to a tall man's beard; the point of a shirt collar poking at my chin; a hand gentle but firm, on my back; my left breast squished just a little; my hand cupping a craggy shoulder blade; fingers spreading over a back, eager to touch and feel.

It's not for nothing that every dance begins and ends in close embrace. It's not just a convention, my friends. It's more than a posture. It's real.

One advantage of having grown up as a dancer here in Buenos Aires is that I take close embrace for granted. I don't question it; I don't get anxious about it; I don't negotiate it. If I'm prepared to dance with someone, I am ready to commit, as fully as I can, to their embrace.

I occasionally encounter people I cannot comfortably embrace because of their stooped posture, jutting heads, caved-in chests or excess tension in their bodies. Some people are hard to get physically close to without contorting your own body. And occasionally I find myself in the arms of someone who constricts me so much I can barely breathe or who digs his right arm into me hard enough to cause pain. And, sometimes, I find my partner standing upright, close to me, and gingerly putting out his hands and barely touching me. It doesn't feel like a real hug. It doesn't feel like commitment.

Being almost afraid to touch at all and gripping, squashing and manhandling may seem like opposites, but in fact the ghost embrace and the wrestler's embrace are two sides of the same coin. They are both physical manifestations of an inability—whether caused by technical problems or anxiety—to engage with the reality of the other person's body. They are both failures of physical empathy, both (probably unconscious) ways of avoiding sensuality. Between scarcely touching and hurting the other person lies the dangerous place, the place of pleasure.

But what usually happens is this: I find myself on the *pista* with a man (or, sometimes, a woman). It doesn't matter who he is: a gorgeous fresh-faced boy young enough to be my son or a grizzled pot-bellied grandpa; a friend with whom I've spent many afternoons on a roof terrace arguing over the minutiae of tango politics; a lover who has explored every fragrant crevice of my body; or a shy and awkward visitor with whom I have no language in common. I put my arms around him as if I were hugging a lover, a father, a brother or a dear friend, with the same gesture that I would use to express real life tenderness. We are not afraid to touch and hold each other. The embrace is a form of communication: I let him know, very clearly that I am *right here*. To read the movements and impulses of his body I get close to him, just like a dog snuffling, so I can feel his dance. It's reassuring, too. It says "I'm with you; we're in this together." It can feel lover-like or collegial, or like two climbers roped together. It's a viscerally pleasurable sensation of warm, human nearness.

I don't feel nervous, vulnerable or exposed. I don't feel that anything I do will be misinterpreted. I'm not wondering what he will think I feel about him or how he feels about me. This is not the moment for that. Right now, it's about the dance. The embrace is the incense that we burn at the altar of the tango gods. It's a sacred hug.

Do I embrace in order to dance? Or do I dance in order to embrace? It's hard to say. The two cannot be separated. But when I embrace – *whomever* I embrace – I embrace them like I mean it.

The embrace as hug

Not every real-life hug is a tango embrace. But every tango embrace, to me, is a real-life hug.

I don't dance with a constant sensation of cuddling and being cuddled, but it's always there in the background, that gesture of affection, with all the neurotransmitters that activates, all the oxytocin, serotonin and testosterone it may send surging through the bloodstream, all the memories and feelings, all the tenderness, comfort, sensuality and sexiness which that can variously evoke and imply.

I was still climbing onto my mother's knee, throwing my arms around her, clinging on like a little monkey and demanding hours of cuddles and dandling of the kind usually reserved for tiny bairns right up to an almost double digit age. I'm the person who sits right down onto the floor, dirtying my skirt, and pets the dog for hours, happily letting my face get soaked by canine saliva; the one who won't move a muscle for fear the cat might slip off her knee again. The person who tends to pet, stroke and nuzzle at the least invitation. The one who is happiest in a cuddle puddle, who hopes the taxi will be crowded so our thighs will squish companionably together, who plants wet smackers on the cheeks of air kissers and tousles the hair of unsuspecting innocents. The first one to grab hold and the last to let go.

So perhaps I am especially susceptible to the power of the embrace. I've always had an extra strong need to be hugged. It can feel soothing and calming. But it can also sneak up on you, take you by surprise and make you uncomfortably aware of needs you were trying to forget you had.

It's always there, that aspect of the embrace, always ready to come to the full forefront of consciousness. For good and for ill.

My need for close embrace

I recently encountered a friend who has been dancing for a long time in a sustained, slightly open embrace. Until now. As the *tanda* began, I felt a deep sense of relief and happiness as he took me in his arms and let me approach all the way till I felt his body touch mine and my arms encircle him in a gesture which I tried to infuse with as much of my real-life affection for him as possible. While I don't want to legislate how others dance, close embrace is profoundly central to my experience. If extreme height differences or raw inexperience make it impossible for my partner, I can live with that. I dance with a lot of partners who open the embrace sometimes, to allow the space necessary for specific moves performed in a specific style (certain types of *giros*, for instance) and I have no problem with that. But if I get the sense that the other person is keeping me physically separated from them for no good reason it gives me a bad feeling at a deep, visceral level. I feel, in some intuitive somatic way, rejected. That sensation never completely dissipates. When they try to play with me in the music, some part of me feels like a sulky recalcitrant toddler. "You don't want to hug me! You know I want you to hug me. It would be normal to hug each other right now. But you won't. Well, I don't feel like playing then."

If you never fully close embrace me (and don't have the excuse of extreme tallness) I will probably never be able to really enjoy your dance, no matter how much musicality, creativity or smooth, beautiful technique you might have.

If you're dancing with a partner and you know you both prefer to stay in an open embrace, of course, that is absolutely fine. But, if in doubt, my advice to everyone is: open the embrace for certain moves, if you like, but always begin and end the dance in close embrace if you want to be sure that your partner will feel good in your arms, if you want to send the clear message: I want to be with you, I want to hold you, I want to dance with you. My friend discovered this. And it changed everything.

Embracing past the height difference

"I prefer dancing with tall women," an acquaintance commented, "because I want to feel *this*." He bent down, put his cheek against mine and snuggled up to me.

The best tango embraces are with people of a similar height. There is a special intimacy in placing your face next to the other person's. For the taller partner, it doesn't feel natural to let someone put their arms around you and place their head against your chest at nipple level while you look over the top of their head. It gives you a strange sensation, as if you are ignoring them.

When you hug someone smaller than you in real life, you bend and place your head next to theirs, you bring yourself down to their level (which would cause back ache if you did it for the duration of a tango). If I want to give a tall friend a proper cuddle, I look for a step to stand on. Neither of these options are practicable in tango. Nor is wearing extra-high heels (one or two centimetres will not make much difference). You've got to stand with good posture, not contort your body, and you need to keep an eye on the *ronda* if you're leading.

But, sometimes, you really want to connect to someone specific, perhaps your boyfriend, husband or lover who is 30cm taller, or someone you have a strong affection for or a shared musicality with – or both.

Although I am happy to leave the tall men, for the most part, for the tall women to dance with (taller followers have the greatest height-related challenges and surely deserve first dibs on the beanpoles) sometimes I don't want to miss out on someone very tall, even if half of their body is in a different time zone. Not all the magic is in the cuddle after all. A great deal of the pleasure has to do with how you hear and express the music and how clearly and sensitively the other person responds to that. And our feet *are* at the same level on the floor.

In tango, not hugging the stranger is strange

In ordinary life, if a man I didn't know grabbed me and squashed me against his chest I would be, at best, taken aback and, at worst, threatened and creeped out. But, in tango, if a man I've never danced with before holds me in an unnecessarily open embrace, or opens the embrace (or opens more than is needed) for a movement which he could perfectly well dance close, I can quickly start getting the heebie-jeebies (unless he's a complete beginner and hasn't mastered close embrace yet).

When this happens to me I can't enjoy the dance. All the way through the *tanda* I am thinking: "*ew!* stop holding me all the way out there! why won't you let me touch you?" As I try to come into contact and my partner repeatedly wriggles away, I feel almost like a sexual harasser, or like Tantalus reaching for the fruit that keeps receding from his grasp.

After experiences like these, when I am truly embraced again – perhaps so close that I can feel his bones individually – I LOVE it. It feels reassuring, clear, present and committed, even chivalrous or comradely. *Here I am, it says; we're in this together.*

The follower who is uncomfortable in your embrace

It's easier to feel when you're leading: the partner who is a little uncomfortable in your arms, politely suppressing an urge to squirm, making little micro-adjustments or holding you so that you are just millimetres away from touching. It can be demoralising. It can make you want to break *tanda,* even if the partner in question is a wonderful dancer.

But, as one who has wriggled in a few embraces myself, I know it's not necessarily a reflection on how the woman (or man) feels about you emotionally or a failure to find that nebulous concept 'connection.' When I do this, as a follower, it's because the leader is holding me in such a way that I cannot get comfortable. Sometimes it's not even conscious. We naturally protect ourselves from postures that feel uncomfortable – and we know where our axis is, how our spine feels and where it feels right to place our weight much better than any leader could.

Some bodies just are naturally incompatible. And some leaders need to work on finding a way of standing, holding themselves, embracing and moving which is more comfortable for their followers and which doesn't provoke that squirmy search for physical ease, those micro-wriggles. It's important to be sensitive to your follower's movements of readjustment. Some leaders are completely unresponsive to my desperate attempts to straighten my spine as they

131

try to bend it in ways a human spine doesn't naturally bend, or to my arm-wrestling fights to prevent them from bending my wrist into a position in which I am afraid it will snap.

It's important to be physically sensitive – but not touchy. Don't play Mr Tango Freud. Don't say "that woman couldn't connect." Don't get upset. Finding a comfortable and functional embrace, posture and coordinated way of moving is a process and you need to take responsibility for your part in it if it isn't working optimally.

When your partner is in pain

It's not easy to adjust your dancing mid-*tanda*. It's one of many reasons that I don't believe in giving unsolicited feedback at the milonga. But there is one situation in which your partner will probably be offering you feedback involuntarily – and you should pay attention. The signs are unmistakable, since responses to pain are deeply intuitive. If you feel her (or him) squirming, wriggling and trying to get free; if she's rubbing her neck, back or wrist between songs; if, between songs, she stands with her head bowed, dejected and unable to meet your eye, make no mistake. That misery is not because she prefers *Villa Urquiza* style, regrets not stepping on the Biagi off beats or thinks your back *ocho* lead is less than ideal. That's pain.

Almost all the leaders I know have tense left arms or squeezy right hands *sometimes*: because they're tired, because the *ronda* is chaotic or just because they're human. I dance with a lot of older men, some of whom are a little less soft and pliant than they were back when The Beatles released *The White Album*. I rarely experience pain – but when I do, there is nothing I can do. But there is something *you* can do, if you suspect *you* are causing your partner pain. Don't get offended, angry or upset. It's a wake-up call. Take it as a signal that you need to change some things about your dance.

First of all: relax your grip. Don't pull her (or him) in towards you so hard, don't clutch her hand so tightly, don't push her arm so hard. It doesn't matter whether you think tango 'requires a strong frame,' 'the man needs to provide energy for the lead' or 'the woman should offer resistance.' It doesn't matter if you can't get a move to work or if you 'need to make sure she stays in close embrace.' Tango should never hurt. Full stop.

If you are unable to relax your grip, the only gracious thing to do is to break *tanda*. And work on your dance. For your own sake as well. Because, when people cannot release their partners from their iron maiden embraces, it's usually because they are carrying too much tension in their own bodies. Check in with yourself: does your back hurt after dancing? Do you feel any aches and pains? Check your posture: are you hunched, or stooped or are your muscles taut? Is there a vein in your forehead popping out alarmingly? If you feel pain yourself, you are probably causing it, too. Some people cannot help causing pain: some people's bear-hugs are a cross between chiropractic and a mammogram; some people don't touch you on the arm to emphasise a point, but punch and hit (an acquaintance once left me bruised after relating a story with particular enthusiasm). For those people, tango might be a way to learn to moderate touch, to find that sweet spot in which you are unafraid to hold and feel, but never cross the threshold to pain.

Followers can hurt their partners too, of course: sometimes by gripping, but more frequently by leaning, draping, slumping and passively forcing their partners to carry part or all of their bodyweight. The same rules apply.

What happens when the follower attempts to choose open embrace

Visitor: I've been dancing for five years now, but I was really confused when I arrived. My teacher [a well-respected dancer] taught us that it's up to the woman how close you embrace. And that it's always an option to stay in open, if you prefer. She said that you can hold onto the man's right bicep, with spread fingers, getting a secure grip there. I thought every competent dancer would be comfortable in both open and close embrace. But when I went to the milongas I didn't get a good response from the men. People told me it "felt strange." A couple of guys asked me what I was doing. And my teacher complained that I "didn't embrace him properly."

Me: However you dance in your local community is completely fine. If you enjoy it, you can do tango steps to speed metal and hold onto each other's earlobes. This is more a question of integration into the wider tango world.

Watch what happens when a *tanda* begins at pretty much any milonga in Buenos Aires and you'll see every couple get into close embrace. The embrace might open later, if they want to dance certain kinds of figures. But watch them walk or do movements which *don't* require a separation of the torsos and you'll see pretty much everyone stay in close embrace.

Many people remain in close embrace throughout: either because that's their style or because the floor is crowded. Watch the dance end – most people will end in close embrace.

It's the leader who generally determines what steps you do. Since whether or not the embrace is close is usually dependent on your choice of step vocabulary, it's the leader, *not* the follower, who decides whether you should be in close or open embrace at any one moment.

You have choices as a follower. When you close embrace, you can put your hand around your partner's shoulders, hold his (or her) right shoulder blade, reach over his right shoulder and down his back a little way, place it lower down his back on the right hand side, etc. These choices might affect the aesthetics of the dance, but they needn't have any impact on the comfort or sensuality. Hold him without constricting his movement in a way that's pleasurable and functional for both of you and it probably doesn't matter where you place the hand (when I'm leading I'm rarely even aware of where the follower's left hand is). Let your fingers fall open or keep them closed – whatever is comfortable for you (my personal preference is for open, with more surface area to touch; but my partner always likes to keep his fingers closed because he feels it's cleaner and more elegant).

Embraces differ. A lot.

But what people *don't* usually do is clearly and firmly hold the other person away from their body without an obvious reason. This is partly just convention and partly to do with the message it sends. It's not so different from real life – if you attempt to hug someone and feel them shrink back it can be disappointing, awkward or even upsetting. It says "I don't really want to be here"; it says "I'm nervous"; it says "I'm not comfortable"; it says "I don't trust you." If you're nervous, that will make your partner nervous. For the dance to work well, you really want your leader to feel calm, confident and secure.

That opening gesture of taking the person fully into your arms, going right up to them, letting your torsos touch, putting your arms around them and being completely physically there with them is very important. Especially for the follower. It says "here I am; I'm with you; this is teamwork; I'm ready for you." That's why almost all experienced dancers close embrace at the beginning of each dance.

Even if I don't know my partner, have never danced with him before or am not sure how well he can dance, I begin, always, by giving him the benefit of the doubt. If I don't want to close embrace him, I won't dance with him. If I can't enjoy being with him in close embrace during the *tanda*, I won't dance with him again – or not until he changes what he's doing. If it's really disastrous, as a last resort I will break *tanda*.

But I'm not going to dance pushing him away. If you do so, you might, like my friend, not get a good response.

Other Partnering Joys and Challenges

You're always limited by your own dance

Me: You danced with *The Seismic Sex Bomb*! Wow! What was it like? How does she feel?

The Slow Semite: It was nice, but not that special. The thing is I'm always restricted by *myself*, by how I dance. I could tell that she had to adjust to be able to dance with me. I know she wasn't able to dance the way she could with someone at her level, because I'm not giving her what she needs.

Me: To really experience someone else's dance, you've got to be a full and worthy partner to them.

On trusting in your partner's enjoyment of your dance

In tango, as in sex, anyone at all sensitive would like to be certain that the experience is as pleasurable for their partner as for them. After a blissful *tanda*, it's natural to ask ourselves anxiously "How was it for him/her?" But, while I wouldn't advocate disregard for the quality of the other person's experience, it is possible to become *too* paranoid about this, to fall into a self-destructive psychological cycle of believing that your dancing sucks, that no one could possibly enjoy it and that you will not be able to give happiness to others on the dance floor until you pass some threshold of expertise or achieve some arbitrary level of technical skill. When you do this, you are postponing the greatest bliss our dance has to offer.

Although it's good to strive for improvement, when you actually get to the milonga you need to put those concerns aside. You need to dance NOW, in this present moment. For almost everyone, at every stage in their dance, there are people you will enjoy dancing with who will also enjoy dancing with you.

There is more than one way to enjoy dancing with someone. I can enjoy dancing with a student because I take pleasure in seeing their progress; with a friend because I love being able to share that with them; with someone with whom I have shared musicality, even if their dance is actually physically uncomfortable to me in some ways.

If they freely accept your *mirada/cabeceo*, please stop second guessing whether they will enjoy your dance. Just give them the best dance you have to offer. Take them in your arms, enjoy their proximity, take joy in the sensation of your body moving in the beautiful idiom of our dance, listen intently to the familiar music – enjoy the moment. This is your dance. Don't apologise for it. Give it your all. Enjoy it. Try to add to the sum total of happiness in the world, beginning with your own.

Adjusting to a new partner at the milonga: some guidelines for both roles

The first thing to negotiate is the embrace. It's an oft-repeated truism that the woman determines the embrace – and it's one I completely disagree with. Unless you're dealing with a very raw beginner who *can't* dance in close embrace yet, always begin by embracing close. Personally, I like to step up to the leader straight on. He (or she) can then choose to meet me straight on, too, if he prefers what we call a two-tit embrace. If he prefers to dance in a slight V, *he* can position his body so that we make contact that way. As a follower, I want to be ready for either possibility and if *I* go straight into a V embrace, I block his options.

Then, for both parties – as in any seduction – begin with gentleness. Start with light contact and little resistance. Never begin by leaning, pushing back or resting your arm on his shoulder with a lot of weight.

I often hear that you should begin by not including any decorations but to me many decorations feel like little smiles made in response to a momentary sense of amusement or pleasure. It's much more natural to let them happen than suppress them. But I don't purposely add extra decorations (in order to give the dance more colour) until I get more of a sense of how he dances: a process which could take seconds or might last an entire *tanda*.

Leaders, begin with simple steps. Keep it simple if you think she (or he) may be a beginner, don't drag her through anything by force. Keep it simple if you think she may be a very good dancer, too: since you are probably better at leading simpler things and she will find that a lot more enjoyable than being led complex things badly. Reserve your complex moves for partners at roughly your own level. When in doubt, wait, pause and feel. Don't focus on making *her* do things or on trying to manipulate her body, but stand up straight and tall and dance your own part of the dance as elegantly and cleanly as possible.

If either or both of you feel off balance, try to find your own axis and your own comfortable balance point. Don't try to readjust your partner's axis. Don't try to pull her (or him) upright or grab her and place her on balance. If you try to guess exactly where another person's balance point is, you are likely to guess wrong (and relinquish your own good posture and stability in the process). Followers, don't hold on to him (or her) for balance. Try to look for balance in your own body's positioning, alignment and relationship with the ground. Don't use the embrace as a lifebuoy to grasp at as you drown. To the best of your ability, if you feel wobbly, loosen don't tighten (relax your grip, allow a little more wiggle room). Pause to let the other person readjust (or readjust yourself). Be aware of your partner, respond to them, but don't attempt to control them.

Finally, if dancing with a new person makes you nervous and you are afraid of making 'mistakes' or misreading leads, then remember that individual errors don't matter at all. It's the overall experience that counts. I've seen many of the top dancers in the world improvising socially and I've seen things going wrong. They smile and laugh it off. It's completely unimportant. This is no time to practise technique – save that for later. Embrace with as much affection as you can muster and focus on letting your movements express what you hear in the music and how it makes you feel. Worry less about whether your partner is enjoying you and try to enjoy them.

When you can suddenly no longer dance

I remember this feeling from skating, years ago, back when I lived in the frozen prairies in the other, northern half of this hourglass continent. One moment I would be gliding smoothly and effortlessly across the lake, far from shore. The next, suddenly, without warning, just when I was beginning to feel at my most confident and graceful, my mittened hands would start flailing at nothing, my body would lurch from side to side and, a second later, I was down. All dignity lost. It was cold, hard and unforgiving.

Tango is like that sometimes, but worse. Suddenly, everything has fallen to pieces. Your legs are two stiff, useless, frozen pillars and all your joints seem to have been dislocated, leaving you a human slinky perched precariously on the edge of a stair. You can never quite find your point of balance, never really come to rest, like a beginner on a unicycle – perched up high, careering along desperately, hoping not to fall. Except that, in tango, you can take someone down with you. Someone baffled, frustrated or even annoyed. *Why are you listing over so far to one side; straighten up and fly right, baby,* you tell yourself. But the more you try, the more things start slipping from your hands, till every moment feels like that moment when you are about to lose control.

There are only two things you can do on a night like that. You can give up and go home. Or you can try to dance through it, if you are lucky enough to have the right partner: a friend come to your rescue, a fellow survivor of the frozen north. With whom it doesn't matter if it feels wobbly, or awkward; who doesn't mind if you are trembly in his arms. Who you feel safe with. Unjudged. Free to dance through the disaster *till you're gathered safely in*. Free to trip and stumble a hundred times and yet still enjoy those rare moments of gliding. Someone who is happy to be out on the treacherous lake with you. If

138

you're lucky enough to find that partner, at that moment, it's pure emotional healing.

Five of the most beautiful words in the language

When one of your favourite dancers looks at you twinkly-eyed and says "I love dancing with you," it makes every penny you spent on lessons, every minute you spent practising your *ochos* through tiredness, every dreary hour rushing across town on packed buses to the practice room or lesson all worthwhile.

"I love dancing with you." It says nothing at all about whether you are a 'good' dancer. You might be a crappy dancer by any objective standard. But at that moment, who cares?

"I love dancing with you." Five of the most beautiful words in the English language. May you hear them often, my friends.

Overdoing the sensuality

I love the sensuality and even eroticism intrinsic to the dance. I enjoy the sensation of being held in a melty *abrazo*. I like rolling through forward *ochos* across the leader's chest in close embrace. I feel comfortable resting my body against skinny chests, muscular pecs, soft squidgy bellies or cushiony breasts. I enjoy playing flirtatious games of footsie in decorations. I like touching skin-to-skin at face level (relative heights permitting). I love the smell of freshly laundered cotton shirts, clean male neck skin and cologne.

But I *only* like to feel the sensuality that is inescapably part of the dance itself – not something tacked on later. Not something you sneak in using the dance as an excuse. Or to try to make it seem extra sexy. At best, that's campy and ridiculous. And, at worst, however innocent your intention, it will give me the heebie-jeebies. I've never enjoyed that aspect of the tango myth which prescribes smouldering looks, abrupt, staccato movements, scarlet and black colours, high slit skirts, pretend kisses and other evocations of the brothel.

I don't like it when the leader's hand wanders up and down and all across my back in an unmistakably caressing gesture. I stiffen up if I feel those wandering fingers creeping closer and closer towards the slope of my arse. Don't suddenly thrust your leg between mine if you're not actually planning to lead a *sacada* or any other move that might conceivably justify that. Thrusting unexpected things between women's legs is a big no-no. No, I'm not planning to sit on your thigh for fun. And don't wrap both arms around me at the end of the song, caressing my upper back with both hands and leaning your mouth in close to my neck.

I won't necessarily assume you are a creep. Maybe you're just trying to add an extra layer of sensuality to the dance. But it's overkill. Sensuality in the dance is a beautiful thing – but only when it develops naturally. When you add it on, I go into self-protection mode. Unless we have the kind of real-life relationship that involves mutual nuzzling (you know who you are), this approach breaks a tacit but important agreement. I let you into my arms to dance. Anything else is taking unfair advantage – and is going to leave me feeling icky.

I had an experience of that kind last night. There might be nothing wrong with what my partner did. It was trivial. I don't feel assaulted or violated in any way and maybe I was even imagining things. I would never want that man prosecuted or punished. But since I like to abandon myself completely to the dance, not spend half my time monitoring the leader's right hand on its meanderings, I'm not dancing with the guy again.

Connecting

It's very different to dance with someone who is just going along with what you want to try to please you or to keep the peace as opposed to someone who *needs* to move to the music in certain ways and who wants to feel what you desire *and* communicate what they desire equally.

You can't connect to someone who isn't fully there.

The playground of nuevo

From time to time I see couples dancing a very classical kind of *tango nuevo* with *colgadas*, *volcadas*, elastic movements, lots of open embrace and unconventional arm positions, *ganchos* every which way and body roll decorations galore. They dance with such sensitivity, so playfully and musically, that I instantly fall back in love with *tango nuevo*.

Their movements seem to be motivated primarily by what feels good (their deeply twisty dissociations looked delicious, the suspended dynamic of their padded walk thrilling) and secondly by a desire to express the music. Whenever there was a choice between aesthetics and expressiveness, they chose expressiveness. Their movements are playful, not necessarily pretty – they even sometimes bordered on the ugly – but they are *always* musical.

On a fairly empty floor, there is plenty of room to move and it can seem natural to fill the space with an expressive dance, unconstrained by the sometimes prissy considerations of *salón* aesthetics. *Nuevo* dancers, to me, are rather like the little girl who had a little curl right in the middle of her forehead. When they are bad, they are horrid. But when they are good, my friends, they are very, very good.

The almost compatible partner

There are some partners with whom everything runs smoothly right away. Then there are others with whom I have serious teething troubles (we have very different training and vocabulary, different step cadences, etc.). Of course, the first category of partners are a great pleasure to dance with.

But I'm most intrigued by, and drawn to, those in the second category with whom it *almost* works. There can be still be much to enjoy in your dance with someone, even if you aren't completely compatible. And if you can take your dance from 'almost working' to '*really* working,' that is a wonderful feeling, even – perhaps especially – when it is challenging to achieve. Those dances help me to grow.

Leading and Leaders

"His walk is so clumsy, uncomfortable and off the music. How I wish he would do a back *sacada-gancho-boleo-soltada* combination instead."

Said no follower ever.

A male friend: I finally managed to get a dance with that leader all the women are so crazy about. He led me for a half *tanda* right at the end. I had been wanting to dance with him for MONTHS.

—Why?

—It was industrial espionage.

* * *

I somehow doubt that many *tangueros*, on their death beds, will say, "My one regret is that I wish I had led more *ganchos*."

* * *

The pleasures of leading

Sometimes I want to put on my slate-grey and businessman-blue leader shoes, to walk firmly and definitely through the music without a single decoration, clean and clear, dividing up the stream of sound with emphatic pauses of varying lengths, like a typesetter adding punctuation, while my partner swirls around me like a soft cloud, a blurry electron field around a nucleus. To feel a partner so soft, fluid and airy that it's like walking through a forest accompanied by a fluttering bird.

Start slow

It's a principle almost everyone pays lip service to, but very few leaders remember when actually dancing: start slow. If you're dancing with a new partner, take a few seconds just feeling her (or his) embrace, posture and way of carrying her weight and let her adjust to you. Then, don't automatically lead a long string of high-energy crazy moves. Don't whirl her round in your fastest *salony* open embrace *giro* or lead her to back *sacada* you; don't start off with a dozen high *boleos* and overturned forward *ochos*; or, even worse, a huge *volcada*. It doesn't matter if the floor is empty and the DJ is playing *El puntazo*.

Begin with all guns blazing and, if she's a less experienced or less skilled dancer, by the end of the song she may be nervous, tense and self-conscious. If *you* are a less experienced dancer than she is, she might well say "thank you" and break *tanda* after one song (most women HATE being manhandled through flashy moves by leaders who haven't mastered them).

But, even if you can tell the moment she embraces you that she's a highly-skilled, experienced dancer and you reckon you are too (a far more dangerous assumption), even if you *could* do a thousand dynamic moves right from the outset, the moves will feel even better if you warm up to them gradually, giving yourself a chance to adjust to each other. You have three more songs to fire your rockets. Don't get your powder soaked in the first thirty seconds.

Think of it like sex. You wouldn't leap upon a new partner and immediately go at them like a jackhammer. Unless you know them and know what they are up for with you, you probably approach intimacy in slow, gradual, tentative stages. If in doubt, keep it in your pants just a while longer.

Why I don't believe tango is about 'showing the follower off'

I often hear leaders say that the point of the dance is to show the woman off, to make her look beautiful or to treat her like a princess. I'm not fond of this image because it seems to imply that the man is not really dancing, just facilitating, enabling, permitting, graciously accompanying or displaying the woman's dance.

When I dance with a man (or woman), I want to feel how they hear the music, how they want to move to it, how they enjoy their own dance, my dance and our *shared* dance. I want to create something together. I don't want to be a diva and princesses have always bored me. I would like an intellectual sparring partner, not a sycophant. Let's take Beatrice and Benedict as our model couple, not Astrophil and Stella. I don't want a monologue when I dance. His *or* mine.

The Leader Thumb Erection

It's one of the great mysteries of tango: the irrepressible power of the leader thumb erection. I know many good leaders who cannot dance unless their left thumb is in an upright position. Curl it back over the follower's hand and watch the dance, like the thumb, grow flaccid and wither. Is the thumb an antenna to receive a signal from above? A symbol of the virility associated with the leader's role (since other turgidities are taboo)? A natural GPS, a sailor's dampened digit held up to test the direction of the wind? An involuntary sign of approval?

I used to repeatedly coax my practice partner's thumb into a supine position, from whence it would spring back up, like a flesh-and-blood Jack in the box, after a maximum of ten seconds. You cannot fight the thumb erection. It is stronger than we are.

But I have come to believe that my officiousness was misplaced and that, in fact, the raised thumb is an arcane rite among leaders, a gesture that honours the tango gods, the equivalent of the taxi driver crossing himself when he passes a church. If it looks like a hitchhiker's solicitous gesture, all the better. Let's hitch a ride together to the place of tango bliss.

The leader as strategist

The role of leader relies on excellent planning. You always have to be literally one step ahead of the game, like a boy scout, always prepared, with each step creating the space you will need for the next, moulding and manipulating the geometry of your relative body positions, like a landscape gardener digging a slope to encourage water to flow downhill *here*, placing pebbles *there* to create an eddy, planting seeds in a neat row *here* in anticipation of later flowering. The secret is so often not in the movement itself but in the preliminaries, in the way you set up the situation, in the careful placing of your body in the movement *before* the tiny drama of the *sacada* or *boleo*. The *mise en place* is more important than the stove.

The leader's movements are often subtler and less conspicuous and therefore need millimetric precision, and constant vigilance over your feet to keep every gesture clean and clear. You have to be as fussy and careful as a man choosing between ten almost identical pairs of black trousers, carefully comparing length of rise and gauging the exact place at which the crease breaks as the trouser leg hits the top of the shoe. The lines we follow must be precise, as clean and crisp as those on a freshly repainted tennis court. Any sloppiness, and everything quickly begins to blur, to merge into a muddy morass of undifferentiated movement in which all figures feel the same.

And there is another, slightly longer term planning necessary too, if, like me, you have fallen in love with the beautiful, elegant sequences of *salón*, if twisting your way through an *enrosque*, stepping into an entrance and painting a semi-circular *rulo* on the ground makes you want to stand up and straighten your tie, if following an eight count figure right through to its end, finishing in close embrace like two singers meandering through their different melody lines to end on the same note, gives you the same deep sense of satisfaction as playing a piano piece flawlessly right down to the final tonic chord. You need to look for the larger structures in the music. You know the violin-driven legato phrase is coming and you're getting into position for a *giro* with *barridas* with swoopy, sweepy *paradas* at the close.

To fit longer figures to the music, you need to think in more expansive terms, in multi-phrase sentences, in more fluid brush strokes, in washes of colour, not just stipples. Until it no longer feels like strategizing, it feels like responding, until suddenly you find yourself in the perfect position to lead that *boleo* and hit the high point in the music, dotting the *i* with the follower's pointed toe. Until you begin the *giro* by intuition *here* and dance the playful double times instinctively *there*, as if the music had planned this for you and you are almost surprised to find yourself perfectly synchronised with it. Until you're no longer thinking *stroke stroke stroke, turn head, breathe* but are just luxuriating in the buoyancy of the water, in the gracefulness of the swimming body, in the pleasures of the wet caress.

Strategists and Tacticians

Two of my favourite dancers form a striking study in contrasts. One is a highly conservative young fogey whose spiritual home is *Villa Urquiza*, clean cut and preppy in looks and dance style, obsessed with elegance, long lines, pretty footwork, classic sequences and fancy figures. The other has a zany crazy *nuevo*-y style in which the follower has to be prepared to be off axis and twisted every which way at any

145

moment and the dance is thrillingly improvised, step by step. Which of them do I prefer? Don't make me choose.

In our dance, there are strategists and tacticians. The strategists have a clear plan. They have figures of eight bars' length which fit perfectly into the melodic phrases and they begin them on the first strong beat of the phrase and continue them until they end, satisfyingly, just as the phrase does, with a clear pause. When that syncopated bandoneon line repeats a second time over, they will repeat the punchy *ocho cortado* they led to express it the first time, neatly tying the different parts of their dance together. They dance in full sentences, in full paragraphs even, in clear sections. One of my favourite leaders dances this way and his dance has a logic to it, a predictability which is not boring—no more than it's boring to hear the tonic at the end of a piece of music—but which is intrinsically pleasing to the somatic ear.

And then there are the tacticians. They adapt to the circumstances on the ground, seizing their opportunities where they can. They don't have a careful battle formation; they're not drawn up in squadrons; they just grab a spare musket and shoot on the run. But sometimes they hit their targets nonetheless.

I love to dance with master strategists. But if you are not good at planning your dance like a chess game, eight moves in advance, if you find you need to change direction suddenly to avoid a surprise enemy ambush, if the music sneaks up on you and is irregular, syncopated or has unusual pauses or if your follower playfully steals a march on you and takes a couple of extra beats to step over after that *parada*—then you need to learn to be a tactician. Ready to change the best-laid plans of mice and milongueros.

Be a master strategist, a Sun Tzu of the dance floor, if you can, if you wish. But be ready, always, for last-minute changes of plan. Equip yourself for guerrilla warfare.

Leaders who don't know their own strength

I've encountered several otherwise excellent leaders (musical, creative, technically skilled) who have led me with an excessive amount of force: gripping me too tightly at certain moments, pushing too hard, adding an extra unnecessary *oomph* to every movement, yelling fit to burst an eardrum when I was ready to respond to a whisper. In the past, I've been tempted to ascribe this to a limited conception of what it means to dance the follower's role or even— against my better judgement—had the sneaking thought that maybe it reflected these men's relationships with women in general.

However, after experimenting with what I'm calling my *follower assertiveness dial*, I found myself digging my heels in (literally at times), offering sufficient resistance to the pressure to move at my own pace, adding my own musical interpretation and even back-leading my own *adornos*. I was surprised—and heartened—to find that almost all the guys in question loved what I'll call my interruptions, my playful rebellions against authority (with only one exception, who was so powerful and forceful that I could do nothing but let myself be swirled around passively, like a straw in a hurricane). The happy responses I got to my interventions, to the pebbles I placed in the stream of strong forceful leading, have made me rethink my attitude.

Men (and occasionally women) who over-lead or strong-arm their partners are not necessarily bullies hoping to dance with marionettes. They don't necessarily aspire to the role of puppet masters. They have just fallen into some bad habits because of poor teaching and learning in that particular aspect of the dance, lack of reliable feedback or too many dances with overly resistant or passive followers (rebellious following is one thing, but mulish stubbornness quite another). Some of them aren't trying, in any way, to suppress the follower's voice.

They are like giant mutts who, in their enthusiasm to lick your face, leap up and punch you in the eye with a huge paw. They have become truck drivers without ever intending it. And would actually love to be mounted on racing bikes instead.

On leaders who 'don't allow you to decorate'

Recently, I was told by three separate women that a particular leader was so dominant that "it's not possible to decorate with him" because "he has a clear plan and you need to wait and see what he wants from you." I found this extraordinary as I had felt, instantly that he was someone with whom I could decorate even more than usual because he was listening very closely to the subtleties of the music and that therefore, when I expressed a musical detail in a decoration, I would be *understood* (a wonderful feeling). And, as so many leaders do, he asked me later "how can I make the women decorate more, play more, be more active?" Like most people with an urge to communicate, he wants a dialogue. ("*All* good leaders ask this," *The Sylph* once said, "'how can I stop her from just following and make her dance?'")

Many of my decorations are slotted into moments when the leader is likely to be pausing anyway. But some are not. They are moments in the music where I take over and make him listen to me. And, likewise, there are moments when the leader will move with a degree of assertiveness (I'm not talking about physical force): "right, now, we're going to step to this rhythm, we're going to dance with this level of tone, we're going to go with this line in the music." As a leader, you can make it clear that right *now* you have a strong need to move in a particular way and with a specific timing and it will only work if your follower comes with you.

Those moments, where one or other person has a pressing and urgent desire to dance to a specific aspect of the music, tend to be among the richest and most interesting moments of the dance. If you want to lead your follower to walk to an obvious rhythmic line or decorate a fill which sits snuggly in a pause between phrases, there is no need for this slightly more forceful communication. It's when you want to do something more unusual or subtler, that you need it.

When I feel this happening with a leader, I know that the leader has something to say about the music. I want to hear him – and also to tell him something in return. It's like my conversations with *The Sylph*. We both talk fast and a lot, but the fact that she has a great deal to narrate and many analyses and theories to offer inspires me and makes me want to share my own stories and ideas. From my perspective as a follower, decorations and play with timings (speeding

148

up, slowing down, pausing unexpectedly) are moments when I am pointing something out to the leader.

It's as though we were on a long country walk together, when suddenly, I stop dead, fall silent, turn my body, widen my eyes and look demonstratively in a specific direction. I have spotted an unusual bird or a small, shy animal. I'm not going to talk and scare it away, but I signal with my body language "look! don't miss it! it's gorgeous!" And the leader, of course, can do the same to me. It's a natural, intuitive thing, outside of tango—calling a person's attention to you in non-verbal ways when you need it. It's only confusing when you are staring into space and there is no bird there. Or when they are short-sighted and cannot spot it or absent-minded and don't notice.

These kinds of subtle, non-verbal communications are easier in tango because you have the other person right there, in front of you: ribcage to ribcage, or, at the very least, holding your hand, touching your back, feeling you. The exact mechanics of this are hard to explain but easy to demonstrate. And, as for the idea that you can't follow in a powerfully active way and imprint your own musicality on the dance if the leader has his own very strong musicality—you not only *can*, but it's the best feeling ever. When the guy dances with attitude, it makes me want to up my game to match him.

Can the follower only play if you let her?

It's a common misconception that, for a follower to be able to play in the music, she needs a leader who will "let" her. That's not true. Playing is neither led, "allowed" nor "facilitated".

There are a couple of things you can do to *stop* a follower from wanting to play: have a pause-free, plodding dance unconnected with any detail in the music or, conversely, rush from movement to movement, never allowing her to complete her steps (a technical issue). Or you can attempt to lead and control every last detail, including teeny-tiny steps and follower *adornos*. (Try to lead me to do decorations and you will discover just how stubbornly resistant I can be.) If you do any of those things, she probably won't play—because she'll be in defensive mode, longing for the *tanda* to end.

But, on the other hand, sometimes your follower might not play because she loves the feeling of your led-and-followed, harmonious and connected dance or because the music puts her in a less playful mood. Playing can't be predicted.

You can encourage a very timid follower to become more playful by playing in the music yourself or teasing her by setting up places which invite that, scattering delicious chocolates in her path and hoping she'll take the bait. But be aware that once she gets more confident, she may reject every one of your offerings and find her own.

But you can't in any way 'make her' play. And you don't have to 'let' her. She doesn't need your permission. Playing isn't led. That's part of its nature. Your only choice is how you respond when it happens. Some followers play in a way which is random and unmusical or with such poor technique that they are using you for balance. But if she's really playing confidently, you have three choices. You can get irritated and confused and let it throw you off the serious business of dancing the leader's role. You can simply relish and enjoy it. Or you can pick up a bucket and spade and get into the sandpit with her.

What makes a follower bored of a leader's dance?

Leaders often tell me that they are afraid that their followers will "get bored" of their dance. I certainly *don't* get bored just because a leader uses a very limited step vocabulary. I don't get bored of just walking—that would be like getting bored of kissing. I don't get bored of the *ocho cortado*. I don't get bored of a leader just because he has his own preferred ways of moving, his distinctive way of interpreting the music, his little mini sequences and step patterns, or even his habits and tics. If I love his dancing, I won't get bored of him, just as I don't get bored of my close friends.

When I'm bored, it has nothing to do with how many or how few steps, figures and sequences the leader does or how familiar his dance is but because of an evil incubus which possesses some leaders sometimes, a demon which sucks out their souls and leaves just an empty husk walking to the beat of 1 and 3, stopping like clockwork at the end of every phrase, doing every movement with the exact same timing, feel and quality. I may try from my side of the embrace to put in musicality, feeling and nuance. I am alive. But to no avail: the leader is undead, some tango Dracula has sucked out his soul and I feel that I am dancing alone: even, perhaps *especially*, if he politely and gallantly 'waits' for me to do decorations and leaves space for me to play, like an adult supervising a child in a sandbox. I want a playmate, not a minder.

I'm not bored by what a leader does or doesn't do; but I can be bored by *how* he does it.

Leaders who punch above their weight

You may be punching above your weight at the milonga if you identify with one or more of these:

1. You feel a strong desire to display your entire repertoire of moves to your partner, especially if you are dancing with a better follower.

2. You often find yourself thinking 'wait a minute, how did that move go? What came after the sequence of *sacadas* and the back *boleo*?'

3. You find yourself overtaking a lot of other dancers and/or can only dance in the centre of the floor.

4. People are always telling you to 'just walk.'

5. Older guys at the milonga have asked you more than once to 'calm down.'

6. You learned many of your best moves from YouTube.

7. You find the followers in your local scene 'snobby' and 'cliquish.' It's much easier to get dances with newcomers.

8. Women often gasp, shriek or start reciting Hail Marys while dancing with you.

9. You much prefer dancing with beginners: they trust you and let you lead them however you like. Better followers struggle against what you're trying to do, resist many of your leads and may even break the *tanda*. They've clearly lost the ability to 'let go' and 'just connect.'

Byronic Beginners

I've visited tango scenes in which *nuevo* is still the native tango dialect of the locals, with lots of linear *boleos, ganchos, colgadas, volcadas, soltadas,* etc. And where there is an inverse relationship between how many big, dramatic moves the guys lead per song and how good

151

their dancing is. Places where the beginners are positively Byronic: *mad, bad and dangerous to dance with.*

There are two contributory factors which can often lead to this predominance of gigantic, flashy moves danced any which way among less experienced *tangueros*. One is the music. It could be that the beginners are dancing to lots of Pugliese, interspersed with very dramatic modern orchestras; the grandest, most theatrical of the Di Sarli instrumentals and then – for good measure – maybe even a bit of *nuevo*.

The other factor is space: too much of it. Floorcraft is not an issue in some enormous venues where each couple is dancing in their own gigantic bubble. So people begin with rather manic dancing which calms down a little as they become more proficient. Leaders learn better in more contained spaces.

The leaders that make me feel free

Some leaders are so focused on trying to get my body to do things, so absolutely fixated on me, that they don't look around at what is happening in the *ronda*. I call them *The Puppet Masters*. It feels like having someone grab your arm and help you across a busy road. When you don't want to cross. And the pedestrian light is red. And a lorry is coming.

And some leaders give me a feeling of complete freedom when I dance. It's not just that they are excellent listeners, attentive to my way of moving and sensitive to the subtle somatic indications that betray what I am listening to in the music. It's definitely not that they leave long pauses for me to fill with decorations. (I prefer the time and space for decorations to develop naturally, as a result of the punctuation marks that almost all good dancers hear in the flow of the music and respond to with pauses, suspensions and hesitations in their dance.) What I experience with such leaders is a deeply compatible way of hearing the music and embodying what we hear.

There is, for me, a predictable—though never boring—quality to the timing of their movements (though not necessarily the directions). I feel a pleasing sense of anticipation giving way to satisfyingly fulfilled expectations, just as I do when I listen to the rising and falling arc of a melodic phrase or hear the end rhymes of a sonnet. It's like hearing a poem recited with exactly the intonation I would use or seeing a film of a favourite novel with every actor in the cast looking exactly as I had pictured the characters in my imagination.

Don't get me wrong. I love to watch films of books I've read. I *enjoy* seeing the director's vision; I love being offered a different perspective. I love dancing with people who hear the music differently from me. A partner does not have to be my Platonic missing twin. But it is nevertheless a very special, precious and thrilling experience when the way someone dances feels so right that I have the illusion that I am not following a leader at all.

The leader is there, of course, tangibly present in the lovely softness of the flexible sustained hug which is the tango embrace. I am very aware of him. But I feel as though it's the music, and only the music, which I am following—and, yet, miraculously, my partner is completely with me. Such partners fill me with pure joy.

My different relationship to the music when leading

My favourite thing about leading is the different relationship I have with the music. While, as a follower, I try to express a thousand small details with my free leg in decorations, as a leader I have quite different musical needs. I'm interested in how I can vary the momentum and cadence of my steps, how I can make teeny tiny changes in speed within a beat and, in particular, where I can place pauses. I am choosing where to place the punctuation: a comma *here*; a semi-colon *there*; a clear and decisive full stop *there*. While I am quite a rococo follower and tend to fill every empty space with *adornos*—the music is so rich in detail and I want to dance it all—as soon as I raise my left arm I feel that less is more. I want to be definite, clean and sparse.

The first time I led Caló's *La vi llegar*, a song I must have danced to hundreds of times before, I heard it so differently that I was startled. It was like taking a familiar train journey but sitting on the other side of the carriage, looking at a very different view, coastal path not forest, waves not trees. I was thrilled by the transformation of the familiar into something fresh and different.

Follower musicality is more flamboyant. We hear those triplets and do extra unled weight changes to them; we hear the Fresedo ripples and we tap and stipple; we draw big *rulos* on the ground with the singer's vibrato, we slide our free leg up our standing leg in autoerotic caresses with the sustained notes on the violin.

But the musicality I'm interested in when my *left* arm is raised is different. I don't have as many possibilities for expressive movement; I'm working with a smaller toolbox, so I need to be extra precise to get the message across. I like to ignore all the colouring, crosshatching and *chiaroscuro* and find the outlines of the tango, the beats I want to step on, the structure, the skeleton. I want to leave a lot of pauses. I want to be choosy about the moments at which I move.

Changing the embrace and raising my left arm, I turn from Catholic to Puritan, change from Mozart to Arvo Pärt; from Bruegel to Rothko. I don't want to take too many steps because I want every step to have meaning. And I don't want to make too many movements because I want every movement to be significant.

This discretion seems delightfully masculine (at least, I like to think of it that way). When I dress for the milonga, I open my wardrobe to a kaleidoscope of patterned silks; I choose among a rainbow of options. Whereas, if I were a man, I would be selecting one pair of black trousers with a slightly different waistband and a subtly different finish, with just a little more or less crease, over another almost identical pair. God is in the details. And, after all the froth and frills, all the triplet-hunting and syncopation-chasing of my following, I am longing to pare things down. Leading opens my ears and gives me a different perspective on the music. I recommend it.

Why I often dislike leading men

One of the disadvantages of learning the leader's role, as a woman, is that you quickly come across men who will only dance with you if you are willing to swap the lead back and forth and let them follow from you. There *are* men who are light, responsive and enjoyable followers. But there are also quite a few leaders who suffer from an acute case of Dunning-Kruger syndrome when it comes to following. "You can lead me. Really! I know I weigh 25kg more than you and am 30cm taller, but I'm a *really good* follower."

Being able to follow well is a high-level skill and it's not about being able to do that fancy triple *enrosque*, it's about how it *feels* to your partner. If you are a man following a woman much smaller than you, you need to be especially careful to be gentle, balanced and grounded. If you can't do that, please practise until you can. But practise with other guys, who won't be so easily injured. Pick on someone your own size. And don't claim that you are a "really good" follower. You are giving the few men who *can* follow well a bad name.

Followers and Following

Adorned or plain?

Dear *Terpsi*,

It seems to me, now, that I have to choose whether to be a follower who does *adornos* or one who has a more classic style.

Last night at the milonga, I told one leader that I had been advised not to do so many *adornos*, and he replied that that was exactly what he likes about dancing with me!!

I know that you would advocate doing them, but does this mean that I have to give up on the hope of dancing with the more classic-style leaders? Most of the popular followers really don't seem to do many *adornos*.

Is it feasible to aim to switch between styles (with the danger that the classic leaders will not ask me, if they see me doing lots of *adornos*!!)

Help!

Unsure whether to dance adorned or plain

Dear *Unsure*,

Very few highly-skilled followers do no decorations at all. And very few do a *huge* number of decorations. Most followers decorate with a frequency somewhere in between. Like so many things, it follows a normal distribution curve. There are wonderful dancers who decorate every other step and equally wonderful dancers who decorate once per *tanda*. It's about what you feel confident doing and how you respond physically to the music at that particular moment, with that particular leader, in the course of that particular movement, under those particular floor conditions, on that particular night.

Some inexperienced leaders are taken by surprise by some kinds of decorations. Some beginner leaders don't mind being surprised. Others can't deal with that yet.

With more experienced leaders, I am less concerned, mostly because I cannot think of a leader whose dancing I really enjoy whom I have not seen dancing, often and with pleasure, with followers who decorate exuberantly (if only because there are so many of us out there). Dancing a lot of *adornos* will certainly not stop you from getting dances—if you dance well. I have never noticed a correlation between frequency of decorations *as such* (badly done or unmusical decorations might put people off) and number of dances.

However, there *are* partners with whom I explicitly enjoy *not* decorating, as our specific joint dance just feels better that way or I know that's their preference (it would be perverse to force a lot of *adornos* on someone who definitely doesn't want them).

You cannot please everyone with your dance. So I go on developing my personal dance, which some will love and others will not. One of my strengths lies in my *adornos*. I'm a baroque artist, that's my style and (for now at least) it's what feels natural and authentic to me. So my default option is to decorate a lot.

Practise, play, experiment—find your own dance. But feel free to adjust it to whatever works best with any specific partner.

Good luck!

Assertive following

I like to experiment with the settings on what I call my Follower Assertiveness Dial, i.e. how strongly to let myself express how I am feeling the music—not just in the form of decorations, which can be done lightly, unobtrusively and even sneakily and need not be assertive—but in changes between heaviness and lightness, between luxuriantly slowing down pivots or stomping confidently onto an accented beat before a pause, between letting my free foot drag and whisking it quickly in to meet its neighbour.

It's about conceiving of the dance as musical expression. Once that is your priority, once it's no longer just about the dialogue, the power game, the two individuals and their interpretations, then musical expression no longer causes conflict within the couple because, as long as you are expressing something in the music, it feels

156

intuitive and organic to your partner, not interestingly weird, aggressive or geeky. It makes sense because you are reflecting something that you are hearing and responding to. The leader isn't thinking "*hmm*, what is she doing here?" He (or she) isn't analysing you. He's responding to the music. This requires a commitment to the primacy of the music, and a confidence in each other's musical interpretation: attitudes and skills which are relatively rare in the diaspora, but common in Buenos Aires (where they are highly contagious).

Here, trying to express the music to the best of your ability and showing the other person how you hear it, is not something you might do sometimes, as a follower, if the mood takes you. It's not an optional extra. It's your job.

Don't let timidity stop you from dancing

I often hear followers express a fear that if they decorate or dance expressively and musically, some men won't like it and won't ask them to dance again. Some have even suggested that if you make a mistake or misfollow a lead, you won't get asked again. I also frequently hear "if you say 'no, thanks' to a man you don't want to dance with, other men who see this won't ask you either".

I've known many technically competent and musical women who are too timid, apologetic and anxious in their dance, terribly afraid of making mistakes, of bothering the leader, of being 'heavy' (which carries horribly anxiety-provoking associations for us women) or of doing something 'he might not like.' Some do a few teeny decorations with such cautious gingerliness that they seem to be done with the idea that "perhaps it will be OK, as long as no one notices." Some are so hesitant that they are late for the music (even though there is nothing wrong with their timing when alone). Fear is a very bad counsellor.

Women want to dance. There is often a gender imbalance, which makes this more difficult and, as a result, some become paranoid that they may be rejected or even blacklisted. But a lot of those fears are groundless. A man who doesn't enjoy dancing with me just because I am also expressing the music is a man I probably don't *want* to dance with.

As for mistakes, they create interesting situations to resolve, stimulate improvisation and teach us things about how we like to move, what is natural for our bodies, which of our responses to the music our partner can enjoy, respond to or use. Of course, you shouldn't be obstructive, distracted or sloppy. But if you are unafraid of 'doing something wrong,' if you make your mistakes with confidence and attitude, you can really grow as a dancer.

I don't know any good dancer who wouldn't dance with someone again if the general experience was a pleasurable one, just because there were one or two mistakes. Perfection isn't important, what's important is how the dance felt *throughout* the twelve minutes, not what happened in half a second during the second track when the follower didn't cross when the leader was expecting it. In fact, whenever I've had a musically rich, improvisationally exciting but accident-prone or error-filled *tanda* and I've thought "we misunderstood each other so many times there that he will never dance with me again," I've been pleasantly surprised by being *cabeceoed* again later. That's how unimportant individual errors are.

As for other men not asking you because you declined to dance with their friends—I think that's a misunderstanding of human psychology. How do I feel when someone who I know is choosy about their dance partners wants to dance with me? I feel flattered.

If you let fear dictate your behaviour at the milonga, you will spend a lot of time suffering miserably through dances you don't enjoy (because you don't have the courage to decline). And when someone you *would* enjoy dancing with invites you, they may be underwhelmed if you are mousy, hesitant to express what you hear or don't have the courage to really dance. You will miss out on good dances and suffer through bad ones.

Don't let timidity stop you from dancing!

Playing Together

"When you invite a follower to dance, it's a bit like inviting someone to a dinner party. The follower has come to eat your meal, but she's brought a bottle of posh wine along with her. Are you going to uncork that wine and drink it? If you're the kind of leader who just stops and waits for her to do her thing when she decorates, that's like letting her help herself to the wine, but not drinking it yourself. And if you just ignore her musicality, that's like ignoring the posh bottle of wine and just getting the same old Budweiser out of the fridge." (Laura Balladur)

* * *

"We recited our favourite orchestras, as if we were praying the rosary: D'Arienzo, hit me with the beat; Caló, melt my gold fillings; San Pugliese, break my heart; Fresedo, heal it again."
Michael Griffin, my translation.

* * *

Noelia Hurtado is perhaps the only person ever to wear a very long, very tight pencil skirt to dance at the milonga. With Chicho.

* * *

"I love your Pugliese," one of my favourite partners told me. I am still smiling at the idea that I have a Pugliese that is especially and distinctively mine.

* * *

Like being on really good drugs

I can remember certain *tandas* with extreme vividness years later. What is it that adds that special extra spark, that haunting beauty?

First, most of my really magical *tandas* have been with partners at roughly my own level. Part of the magic lay in my instinct that they were enjoying those dances every bit as much as I was, that we had each met our perfect match.

Secondly, more importantly, there was so much shared musicality that every movement felt intuitive. Which doesn't mean that I couldn't be surprised, but it was the delighted surprise of someone who understands that the solution to a problem has been staring her in the face all the time, a surprise of "of course! that makes perfect sense!" Coupled with a complete confidence that everything I tried to say, somatically, about how I heard those tangos, would be deeply understood. Even when it came as a surprise to my partner.

I can remember pausing to decorate a rather subtle element of the music as I was about to dance a forward *ocho* and my partner said, quietly and meaningfully, "*aha!*" – a perfect example of the musical surprise that is instantly comprehensible to the other person.

That, above all, makes for a really memorable *tanda* – that sense of being musically understood. Or, as a friend puts it, "when two really musical people find each other, it's like being on really good drugs."

Copycat decorations with Mr Wiggly Bottom

It's one of my favourite things in the world: what I call the copycat decoration. To produce the effect, as a follower, first wait for the first of two repeated playful little phrases in the music—especially if they have some obvious offbeats or syncopations. (Donato is ideal, but Troilo-Fiorentino has many, too). In music, something that is said once will almost always be repeated a second time later. Add an even number of tiny little stuttery extra steps, unled weight changes or very obvious tap decorations to express the rhythm of the first phrase. Then, later, when that phrase repeats, suddenly stop expectantly, pause just a little longer than necessary, ground yourself as if expressing an unwillingness to rush off anywhere. And feel the leader copy your earlier decorative movements. It's almost like yodelling into a canyon: the echo will inevitably sound. Your pause at the end of the first phrase is like the pitch of your voice rising at the end of a question; it invites a response and most sensitive partners will offer one. In tango, a space is an invitation. When our partner opens a door, we step confidently inside. Opportunities for a follower to be the one gallantly holding the door ajar are more limited, but this is one of them.

Copycat decorations feel especially delicious with *Mr Wiggly Bottom*. The rest of the time, his hips are well behaved, his pert little bottom glides smoothly along with ne'er a twitch, while his face is taut with concentration and his walk is elegant and *salony*. But lead one of those rhythmic decorations and invite him to follow suit and you will feel a wibble wobble, a tremor, subtle but unmistakable. His signature botty tremble. A distant echo of belly dance.

Helping interpret the music

"You really help me interpret the music," a leader told me last night. In one sense, this is what a follower always does: we always create an interpretation of the music together. But it also touched on another issue: dialling up the volume on the follower's input into the musical interpretation, beyond *adornos* (though *adornos* too are part of that input). Of the things I do as a dancer, this seems to receive the most positive responses, and arouse the most (mostly positive) surprise: slowing down and (though it's more difficult) speeding up movements unled, playing with the timings of my responsiveness, being assertive about pauses. Playing not with space—I'm not deciding on directions, specific movements or figures—but with time.

Like most forms of play, it has risks. If you sharpen your ears for your partner's interpretation of the music and try to coordinate precisely with him, you stand a greater chance of being completely together, achieving a smooth harmoniousness and finding a flawless, seamless dance. As a follower, to take an initiative musically is to take a risk. I once had a partner stop dead and remain frozen to the spot through two phrases of a fast D'Arienzo because he was so startled. Such instances are rare, but can't be completely ruled out.

Once you are not just attempting to reproduce the timing of what your partner is proposing—perhaps with decorations thrown in where the dance allows space for them—you have a dilemma: how to calibrate your dial when it's not automatically fixed at close to zero. Where to find the balance between listening to his interpretation and offering your own. There are likely to be hiccups, small unevennesses of texture, momentary indecisions and awkwardnesses until you get the balance right.

In fact, it feels the most nourishing when there is that roughness of texture because it's part of give-and-take. It's not as fun if the leader is very dominant and (not necessarily consciously) resistant. Then it can feel as though you are being very aggressive in trying to make your voice felt—even if the leader himself seems to be relishing your assertiveness. And it's *definitely* not as fun if the leader is completely receptive, never proposing timings back, with a hair-trigger responsiveness to everything you do (you may find yourself tempted to take over completely and that feels lonely and empty, since those proposals are meant to become part of something shared). It's a flirtatious thing. You ideally need someone who flirts back.

But the risks are worth it. In the diaspora, this form of dancing seems to be uncommon—I often hear people saying things like "most leaders don't get to feel this"—and I constantly hear positive feedback about it (though, to be fair, perhaps some people hate it but are too polite to say so—the riskiness of this strategy can't be eliminated). Perhaps only those to whom it is a novelty feel the need to comment.

Part of the follower's role is mirroring. It can be very fulfilling to just be a good listener. If you copy your partner, you can more easily match him. I don't want to relinquish that mode forever. But when you put away the tracing paper, hold your pencil freehand and start creating your own sketch, that's when some of the real fun begins. Things get a little messy: sometimes you colour outside the lines. But the artwork is the richer for it.

Over-decorating and not sorry

As we danced the Pugliese instrumentals I pulled out every last *adorno* I could think of—and tried to do them with a degree of power, since I know that partner well and he loves loves *loves* it when followers are assertively playful. I stroked a foot up the outside of his leg, up the lower part of the inside of his leg (he actually squealed with delight), tapped his feet and ankles in every conceivable position, with both feet, added a thousand extra unled teeny tiny steps and mid-step weight changes, drew tiny circles on the floor (it was crowded), delayed my pivots and took my own sweet time in finishing my forward *ochos* and even, at one point, wiggled my bottom a little. All in the service of letting him know that I was really feeling the tug of the Pugmeister's powerful *whoomphy* pulse and the bitter sweetness of his violins. I'm pretty certain it looked campy and ridiculous. But when the *tanda* ended he said one emphatic word in a voice that sounded like a Harley Davidson revving. "*Phwoarrrr!*"

The pleasures of dancing milonga

In fast milongas, there isn't time to wait for the lead or to work out exactly what points in the music your partner might want you to step on. You have to take an executive decision: be intuitive, definite and fast. You've got to press the red button and shoot your missiles first. You've got to pounce on those fast notes with confidence, trusting your leader to be with you. You've got to be cheeky, flirtatious, daring and bold.

You've got to root yourself firmly into the ground in those pauses, too. They aren't hovery, floating moments where you suspend your movement, but are ready to resume motion at a moment's notice. No. They are big inky full stops stabbed into the page at the end of each sentence. *Rush rush rush rush* HALT. It feels a little risky. There is always the slight possibility that he will stop and you will continue or vice versa (one or two beginner men have actually body checked me when I was pausing at the end of a phrase in milonga and their momentum carried them onwards).

There's always a risk that you'll choose wrong and end up out of sync. But it seems all the more magical when it doesn't happen. When the milonga is over and you were together throughout, twin synchronised divers breaking the surface together. In the warmest, most harmonious close embrace, but with wild, frenetic, flickering feet: a lake of calm above, a sparky fire below.

The magic gnome and the metamorphosis

"You remind me of Noelia when you dance," favourite partner *The Magic Gnome* once told me. After I recovered from the narcissistic head-rush and decided that perhaps I wouldn't instantly commit suicide after all (in order to die at the moment of maximum happiness) I realised that—while I am nothing like Noelia, objectively speaking—this does make a certain kind of sense. While every dancer is an individual with his or her own personal style, there are familial resemblances between leaders who are aficionados of different styles and between followers when they are dancing with those leaders (in most cases, we followers are chameleons who change the shade of our scales to match our partners, with no fixed allegiances to any particular school: leaders are monogamists; followers are polyamorous). Each style has its role models who encapsulate that way of dancing.

I have never taken a lesson or workshop with Noelia and Carlitos. Instead, I take lessons in *salony Villa Urquiza* style and partner a calm *salony* boy who spends hours every day practising his *enrosques*. But I consider rolling close embrace a style: a school, a tendency, a grouping. Carlitos and Noelia are its most famous protagonists. And, within that style, a certain posture, embrace, way of moving, type of dissociation, and even footwork and use of decorations, make sense. It's a system and has emergent properties.

If you dance a little bit like Carlitos, I'm going to naturally dance a little bit like Noelia (with a certain familial resemblance, just as the bulbous-nosed, pot-bellied uncle and the beautiful gazelle-like supermodel niece both have the distinctively-shaped family eyebrows and the characteristic dimple in their left cheeks). That's what will fit your dance. I'm not Shakespeare, but when I write Shakespearian sonnets I feel part of a tradition in which his work is the model. Likewise, when I dance rolling close embrace, Noelia is the master practitioner who comes instantly to mind. In the arms of *The Magic Gnome*, I feel like her long-lost sister.

Dr Singletandaman

Possibly my favourite consecutive *tandas* ever happened in New York. At the time I visited, it was the norm for people to dance two *tandas* at a time. A friend of mine, however, only ever dances in single *tandas*. "I like to optimise my experience," he told me, "to try to find the best partner I can for every orchestra." I had just danced with him and we returned to our different perches as the *cortina* sounded. And then I heard the opening notes of a lush Pugliese-Chanel number. Pugliese is my favourite orchestra and *Dr Singletandaman* is my favourite person to dance to it with locally. I felt a sudden intense

164

frustration at having missed my chance, since we had just danced—and an energetic milonga too. My eyes intuitively wandered in his direction, even though I knew I couldn't dance this with him. And then, to my surprise, he *cabeceoed* me and, with great glee, I rushed over and grabbed him and uttered a deep and most undignified sigh of pleasure. Being in the arms of a good dancer when the opening bars of a Pugliese sound is like getting the last beautiful silk dress from the sale rack and finding it fits you like a glove; like leaping onto the Eurostar at the last moment—and being upgraded to first class. Free champers, and Paris. Let's go!

Feeling the way your partner hears the music

"I don't usually like these slow *Guardia Vieja* songs," he said, after we had just danced to my favourite OTV track (*Coqueta*), "but I can tell that *you* like them and that makes me enjoy them too." It was one of my three favourite moments at *El Motivo* one night, all three of which involved somatic communication – feeling the way my partner hears the music.

In another partner's arms, I immediately felt that he wanted to race through the songs. Not rush, but sustain a flow of satisfying speed. And then, as he led me into a *parada*, I slowed right down, delayed my arrival, like a human lasso slowly knotting around a post and felt him, instantly, soften, calm and feel the stretchy legato with me. Then, just as I fully arrived, the tension was broken, the spring was released, I felt the engines purr and *Speedy Gonzalez* and I sped joyfully through a lovely, whirly *giro*.

Later, with a different partner, dancing to D'Arienzo, as the mellow violin countermelody began, I smoothed out my steps, put away the taps and flicks of my little staccato decorations and, perhaps it was coincidence, but as the next violin solo began, this time he led me to a *parada* and I let my free leg caress his in careful time with the opening notes of the fiddle.

My favourite thing of all about tango is feeling how another person hears the music and knowing, when I express how I hear it, that they are listening. It's a constant conversation which is stimulating but not tiring—listening to someone talk forever and speaking back yourself, without ever getting exhausted by all the words or needing a break from the chat. As a friend put it, the tactile/kinaesthetic interaction gives us energy, rather than sapping it. It combines all the best qualities of a restful, companionable silence and a need for personal communication into a special kind of dialogue through movement, in which the subtlest of hints will be understood. Music makes the body eloquent. And when we dance we put ourselves into a state of intense receptiveness, a deep listening in which the quietest whispers won't go unheard.

Camping it up

We both tried to decorate at once, feet whirling in our shared space beneath the embrace, so that we knocked calves for a second. '*Bwaaahahaha!* We both have crazy legs!' he told me. Later, I waited in a very solid, rooted, I'm-not-going-anywhere-no-matter-what-till-the-music-tells-me-to pause until Di Sarli just lightly touched a note on his keyboard, pianissimo, and then I gently tapped his ankle. 'Genius!' he laughed. And then I did my characteristic leg caress decoration, in a low, slow stroke, high up the INSIDE of his leg. 'Whoa!' he exclaimed and I glanced at his face to see him biting his lower lip and widening his eyes in an exaggerated pantomime of arousal. And then the tango ended and he threw us suddenly into a stagey posed *quebrada*, gazing at me with a sultry expression.

I love dancing with gay boys. I have never met one who thought a woman decorated too much or was too playful or flamboyant. Campiness, in dancing and life, can be theatrical and insincere. But sometimes it also frees you to express what you are feeling with a courageous brazenness. Sometimes you need to throw all restraint to the winds and go for the full-fat version. With extra whipped cream.

Dancing straight off the plane: odd distortions of time and space

Sleep-deprived and woozy after thirty-six hours of complicated travel, I was little shaky on my pins when I first took to the dance floor, a little uncertain of my axis. But soon I felt a growing confidence, the floor felt reassuringly firm underfoot after being bumpily airborne and my body stretched and twisty after the cramped origami of the airplane. I was reminded of the words of the tango, "how good it is to dance on solid ground."

And then that strange magical thing happened: the milonga distorted time in puzzling ways, stretching it *here*, like invisible chewing gum, scrunching it up into a fist-sized wad and tossing it into a wastepaper basket *there* in a strange temporal relativity that defied Einstein. Perhaps it was because of Avik Basu's wonderful music choices: the intense Di Sarlis and D'Arienzos, the dramatic sung Puglieses and De Caros leavened with lovely OTVs and bubbly-textured Fresedos. When I paused at the end of a phrase or to mark an accent in the music, I felt as though I rested calmly there for ages before moving off. When I lifted and twirled and tapped my free leg in *parada*, I seemed to have months of time to deliciously linger. And yet the *tandas* were over too fast. The De Caros (my favourite *tanda* of the evening) sped by like a flock of swift-winged birds. And the milonga itself was over in the blink of an eye. One moment I was dancing my first *tandas* of the night. And the next *La Cumparsita* was sounding, to my utter amazement. "What?" I exclaimed to my partner. "It *can't* already be over!"

But outside my window the velvety black of the Oregon sky is turning the pale grey of a banker's business suit and I'm left only with the memories of lovely embraces, with *all the strength and all the sweetness rolled up into one ball*, condensed into my glass of Malbec, into a sentimental tear welling up in my eye (or is it just tiredness and thickly-applied mascara?). *We cannot make our sun stand still. But we can make him run.*

Musical Partner Play

Syncopations in Troilo

There are many emphatic and sometimes irregular and misleading syncopations in these fast Troilos and dancing to them has turned into a game. "*Shit*," my partner exclaims, laughing, as he misses one. "Oh, I don't know this one," he says, at the beginning of the next song, and I can feel him focusing in on me; he knows I know these tangos by heart, I can step on the syncopated beats from memory. He follows my movements, we dance together through the syncopations. And within half a song he has got the hang of how they work and is pouncing on them gleefully with me, no longer needing my somatic indications.

He erupts in momentary laughter when one escapes him and he treads with stompy decision into a moment of musical calm. It's like a child learning language: in places he parrots to get a feel for it and then, very quickly, starts to recognise and play with underlying rules, occasionally getting them wrong (just as a young child will say "I singed," their mistake demonstrating a grasp of the rules as to how the past tense is formed). He is extremely musical (I only have, temporarily, the brute force advantage of memory). He's a dancer who enjoys playing with the music and a leader who allows the follower's musicality to inform and enrich his own. Be a leader like him—and you will go far.

Contagious musicality

My friend Paul Akmajian and I once gave a class on a very simple double time *corrida* figure. We decided to show the students where in the music we like to place it by putting on a Donato track, walking to it and inserting the little *corrida* wherever we felt the music suggested it—both at once but, crucially, not in a couple, but *solo* (dancing round the room, each alone).

To my surprise and the students' bewilderment we chose to insert the double time walk at completely different points in the music. I don't think we ever coincided in our ideas of where to dance the *corrida*. And yet Paul is one of my favourite partners precisely because I feel I can interpret the music so freely and intuitively when I'm dancing with him.

Tango is about shared, transmissible musicality. It's catching: like the giggles, infectious, like an auditory chickenpox. In the embrace, focusing intently on the small movements of the other person's body, we are deeply suggestible. At an unconscious level, I can feel my partner making little muscular preparations and micro-adjustments to the tone of his (or her) upper body as he prepares to move to the rhythm of the bandeoneons; I can feel him getting ready to pause in a lovely suspension as the solo violin soars or to pursue some fast triplets on the piano and, at once, I not only hear what he hears, but feel I want to dance to that too.

Often, I don't know who noticed that moment in the music first. Who started it, him or me? Who chose to step to those triplets, to slow down the *giro*, to give the *boleo* that precise timing?

"Of course," one of my students commented, "if you're clever, you can make the man think it was his idea." Indeed. And vice versa. We use our bodies to turn up the volume on certain aspects of the music and suddenly the other person hears them and responds.

I have never felt that someone was musical but incompatible with me because they had a different way of hearing the music. Almost anyone who is really focused on the music can make you hear it too. Can make you feel—with delicious narcissism—not just "oooh, how musical *he* (or *she*) is," but also "*ha! (polishing fingernails on breast pocket)* how musical *I* am!"

A milonguero who walks on the pulse

His eyes, twinkly amid a mass of concentric laughter lines, like mountain lakes on an Ordnance Survey map, catch mine for *cabeceo*. He holds me in a bear hug of an embrace and we are away. He steps on the pulse throughout and leaves no pauses, not even at the ends of phrases. He is like a big, burly, swinging metronome. When there is space, he walks. And when there isn't, he twirls me around with him in a *milonguero*-style *giro* or two and perhaps an *ocho cortado* if he is feeling inspired. So why is this smiley, bulbous-nosed, twinkly-eyed teddy bear of a dancer one of my favourite partners?

He provides a really clear, reassuring framework, a structure which I can fill with music. It's always clear when he will step and so, in the space I know I have, there is time to accelerate or slow down a tiny fraction, time to stomp on the beat with a heavy tread or pad as softly onto it as a cat, to paint the intervening space and time with flicks and stipples, to subdivide the beat into a few extra steps— skipping happily through three small steps where he led just one. It's like being on a climbing frame in a school playground, a frame whose geometric solidity makes me feel safe to do somersaults and dangle from the bars like a monkey.

I remember my mother painting by numbers (literally) when I was a young child. One of my earliest memories is of her drawing a grid on the canvas, ruling vertical and horizontal lines in pencil. Once that was done, she grabbed her pallet knife and oil paints and the fun began. This partner is the generous draftsman and I'm the smearer of paint.

We often consider walking on the pulse throughout the song to be a very basic, even primitive, way of being musical. And it *can* feel mechanical and boring. But sometimes it makes perfect sense. There's a reason, after all, that when we hear music we tend to seek out the basic underlying beat and stamp our feet, jiggle our legs, tap our fingers on the table and move our heads back and fro to it. The pulse can be powerful. I love filling that framework with music.

Beating

When two people sing pitches which are *almost* identical, but not quite, the overlapping patterns of sound waves produce a wailing *waw-waw-waw-waw* sound which musicians refer to as 'beating' and which sounds highly unpleasant to a trained or naturally pitch-sensitive ear. While there is no equivalent term for a dancer stepping ever-so-slightly out of time with the music, there really *ought* to be because there is definitely a somatic equivalent of 'beating,' a wailing, jarring, out-of-rhythmness. If you are dancing with someone like that, it feels the way someone with perfect pitch must feel, trying to sing in a choir with many singers who are flat.

A leader like that must feel me 'rushing' at times, 'resisting' at others, as my body naturally tries to move with the music. I don't have a dancer's equivalent of perfect pitch—I'm much more fallible than that. But I can't un-hear what is happening in the music; I can't ignore it; I can't un-know where the rhythms fall. (I'm not talking about different musical interpretations. A well-trained follower will feel and respond to the leader's choice to emphasise the staccato instead of the legato, the off beats, etc. The problems come when the leader isn't actually dancing to anything in the music).

Here are some signs that you might be subjecting your follower to an out-of-rhythm or even rhythm-deaf dance:

1. You have no idea what orchestra is playing, nor do you care. (Aren't they all more or less the same anyway?

2. You've never understood what *cortinas* are for.

3. You get to the end of the dance and realise that you didn't pause at any point.

4. That complicated figure with the little double time *corrida*, the overturned back *ochos* and the *volcada* miraculously fits any point in any tango.

5. You hate it when women do decorations—it's so confusing. Why is she doing three little triplet-speed taps with her free foot right now, for instance?

6. At certain points in the song your followers tend to stop moving and you end up tugging them, running into them or tripping over them.

7. You've never understood what people mean when they talk about dancing differently to violin melodies.

8. Tango music is really boring; you hear enough of it at the milonga. You're certainly not going to listen to it at home.

9. It's really difficult to predict when a tango is going to end. Yours usually end with a couple of stumbling steps and "*oops!* sorry!" Sometimes the follower has to stop you because you didn't realise the music had ended and you still hadn't finished that *corrida-ochos-volcada* figure.

10. You've never understood why so many good dancers, who surely have lots of flashy moves up their sleeves, dance so many *salidas*.

If this is you or someone you know, there is hope. Buy them (or yourself) attendance at a seminar on musicality (I recommend those given by Joaquín Amenábar, Victor Simon, Ramiro Gigliotti, Alex Krebs, Theresa Faus, and Michael Lavocah). If there isn't one locally, demand one. And read Lavocah's book *Tango Stories: Musical Secrets*.

Fiddle faddle fiddlesticks

Dear Leaders,

You know those little rapid runs on the piano or bando, very fast syncopations, musical decorations, 'fills,' 'breaks' or what I like to call the twiddly bits of the tango? Have you noticed that very few of the best leaders actually try to lead steps to those moments in the music?

Those little moments are places where the follower can bring out her delicate, pretty, fast decorations (it's much easier to decorate those moments than to lead and follow them). They provide her with an easy way to participate in the musical conversation.

If you lead, lead, lead, lead through the whole song, including those little fills, you are drowning out her voice, like a person who won't let their interlocutor get a word in edgeways. If you drone on like that, dominating the entire conversation, she is likely to zone out.

The leader's and follower's relationships to the music and choices about what to express are different—that is part of the charm of our asymmetrical dance.

There *are* exceptions to this (as to every rule). Little weight changes on the spot, for example, are easy to lead and follow and can work well in those 'twiddly bits'—in *moderation*. Leaders can decorate, too, and, in fact, one of my favourite things to do is alternate copycat decorations (you take one phrase, I'll take the next).

But, dear leaders, if I avoid your eye when the Rodriguez *tanda* sounds, if I look bored and frustrated when I'm led to do fussy little steps during runs, it's because it (a) feels blocky and awkward and (b) stifles dialogue between us.

And if you do this to me during the D'Agostino *tanda* – unless you *really* know what you are doing – I will be wishing a slow, painful death upon you. A death that resembles the suffering you are putting me through with your twiddly fiddle faddle. Death by a thousand cuts.

The Appeal of the Classics

I never get bored of certain tangos, even though I dance to them almost every night: for example, Di Sarli's *Nada* and *Cosas olvidadas*, D'Agostino's *Tres Esquinas*, Troilo's *Te aconsejo que me olvides*, Fresedo's *Buscándote* and others. If I listened to any non-tango track even 1% as often as I listen to those, I would be heartily sick of it. But this music never seems to get old. In the same way as dancing a back *ocho* never seems to get boring. The music and the movements are tiny universes with ever more elements to explore.

It's fun to discover tangos which are new to me or be pleasantly surprised by seldom played gems. But they generate a different level of emotional intensity from those classic songs we have danced to at a thousand milongas, which have gradually built up layers and layers of emotional charge.

n I hear Pugliese's *Fuimos*, for instance, no matter where I
n close my eyes and be instantly transported to *El Beso* on a

172

Sunday evening in the arms of one of my favourite partners. Those classic choices are infused with memories both mental and somatic and you don't even have to listen to them consciously with your ears: your body knows them note by note, your legs respond and you can ride the feeling and let muscle memory do the rest.

Twelve-minute miniature heavens

The many different satisfactions to be found in the twelve minutes of a tanda

There is the pleasure of swapping the lead back and forth with a female friend and feeling, gradually, step by careful step, a *salony giro* with entrances, *enrosques*, *lápices* and *barridas* taking shape within you, in your flat shoes, with your left hand raised. At first, it's panicky and jerky – "oh my God, now I'm *here*, quick, better step in; better change weight; better paint a *rulo* before it's too late" – but later the figure bears the ease of a leader's calm anticipations, as you prepare each movement one step in advance, like a Scrabble player shuffling your letters into position on their stand, waiting for your turn so you can confidently lay them out on the grid and make the sense you planned.

There is the pleasure of being led through a hundred smooth *giros*, corkscrewing through a set of intrinsically beautiful movements, slinky as a leopard. There is that snaky feeling of dissociating together, mirroring each other's spirally movements, like tracing flower petals with the round cut-out of a plastic school stencil. The mechanism working in your body, your back moving first, your free leg trailing behind can feel so wonderful that you deliberately focus on technique for a moment, just to relish the sensation of conscious competence.

There is the pleasure of catching the fast D'Arienzo piano notes in a flurry of weight changes and feeling your partner take up your suggestions and dance them with you, giggling with delight.

There is the pleasure of being in the arms of one of the most creative and energetic of leaders, knowing that you have to be attuned to the slightest signal, primed, feet on the starting blocks, heart racing, ready to sprint. It's like being part of a thrilling tennis rally that keeps the ball travelling between you seemingly for ever as you duck, dive and grapevine across the court. It has all the thrill of competition, without the danger of losing and with the score always at *love all*.

There is the pleasure of dipping into the cool of these babbly, burbly Fresedos and proudly bursting the ethereal soap bubbles of their triplets, time travelling in your imagination and connecting with those long-dead musicians, because the only time is now and *now* we are hitting those lovely emphatic triplets together and that's the only simultaneity that matters.

There is the pleasure of holding someone just because the comforting firm flatness of their chest feels good against your body, reminding you that this place, next to a man, is a place you are unavoidably drawn to.

These are sensations which I don't think I will ever tire of, anymore than I would tire of a rich velvety Italian espresso on a crisp morning, the feeling of silk against my freshly-waxed legs or the taste of a French kiss.

From the intellectual to the sexual, through every possible gradation in between, tango is like a shell world in which we inhabit every layer at once: here, the consciousness of the lovely syntax of steps, the grammar of movement and the beauty of figures; there, the séance with thirteen dead musicians, summoned by a Faust with a MacBook; here, the feeling of friendly one-upmanship ("you want that *ocho*? I'll give you that *ocho* back—with interest!"); there, the dreamy floating in an oxytocin sea, luxuriating in the body and its pleasures, cravings and needs.

Glossary

Rather than being hard and fast definitions, these explanations reflect my own understanding of some of tango's characteristic features.

Adornos (lit. "decorations"): See *decorations*.

¿Bailás?: While, at many *milongas* and *prácticas*, invitations to dance are offered, rejected and declined through eye contact and subtle gestures (see *cabeceo*), verbal invitations are possible in some situations, too. In Buenos Aires, most people ask using the one single word *¿Bailás?* (lit. *Are you dancing?*)

Bandoneon: A type of squeezebox or accordion with buttons on both sides, the *bandoneon*'s plangent notes are probably the most characteristic aspect of tango music. Originally a German church instrument, the *bando* was brought over to Argentina in the late nineteenth century. Not originally designed as a melody instrument, the *bandoneon* is fiendishly difficult to learn to play.

Barrida (lit. "sweep"): A movement in which one dancer uses their free foot to sweep the other dancer's free foot along the floor. Can be performed in a straight line, or as part of a *giro*.

Boleo: A movement in which the leader changes direction to create a momentum which causes the follower's free leg to swing out along the floor (a low *boleo*, sometimes called a *planeo*) or, with higher energy, into the air (a high *boleo*). The change of direction can be performed during a straight step (resulting in a linear *boleo*) or during a turning step (resulting in a circular *boleo*).

Cabeceo ("head signal"): At more traditional *milongas*, men invite women to dance by catching their eyes and signalling to them from their seats, generally at the beginning of the first tango of the *tanda*. This is usually done by cocking the head or making another subtle gesture. If the woman nods her acceptance, she then remains seated while he crosses the room and comes to stand in front of her chair.

Caminata: A figure based on walking, usually with a series of small, quick steps. If fast, this is sometimes called a *corrida*.

Chamuyo: The spiel men often use when chatting up a woman or trying to pick her up.

175

Close embrace: A way of dancing in which the dancers' torsos remain touching throughout. Almost all experienced dancers walk and perform simple moves in close embrace. Depending on their chosen style of dancing, they may then open the embrace to enable them to dance specific moves which require a slightly greater distance between the couple. As dancing in *close embrace* is such a beautiful feeling, usually the embrace will be opened only as much as is necessary for the chosen move and closed again afterwards. See also *embrace*.

Colectivo ("collective transport"): a city bus.

Colgada: See *tango nuevo*. This is not exclusive to *nuevo*, but I've defined it there for simplicity.

Comme Il Faut: As well as being the name of a tango, this is an expensive, iconic and undoubtedly sexy brand of women's tango heels. Known for their vertiginous heel heights (10cm for the highest shoes), which have since been adopted by most other brands.

Competitions: Unlike ballroom dancing, tango is not generally danced competitively and there are no widely-recognised tango qualifications, either for performing or teaching. The one really important international tango competition is the *Mundial de Tango*, held once a year, during the month of August, in Buenos Aires. The initial rounds are held at *milongas*. Couples compete in two strictly-defined categories: *tango escenario* and *tango salón*. The kudos obtained by winning the *Mundial* can result in a very lucrative performing and teaching career for the successful couple. The other important tango competition is the *Metropolitano*, held in Buenos Aires in May.

Corrida: See *caminata*.

Cortina: See *tanda*.

Decorations: Movements, usually small and subtle movements of the feet, which are not led and followed. They can occur at pauses in the leading and following (including micro pauses) or during a led-and-followed step. Followers usually decorate more than leaders. Decorations are often seen as a chance for the individual dancer to express subtleties in the music which are too fast or delicate to easily lead steps to.

Diasporans: My term for people who dance tango primarily in communities outside Buenos Aires.

Dissociation: This is when dancers move one body part independently of another or, most commonly in tango, initiate a movement in one part of the body, so that movement in another part of the body is delayed. In tango, it most frequently refers to the way in which dancers turn. While ballet dancers often turn the entire body as a unit – lifting up onto their toes and forming one tight, twirling column – tango dancers almost never turn *en bloc*. Instead, most dancers will initiate the turning movement from the torso, first twisting the torso towards their right, for example, and then allowing the lower body to follow, turning the hips and letting the feet pivot on the floor. This produces a corkscrewing action which is highly characteristic of tango movement. Movements usually begin in the upper body because that is where the dancers have physical connection, through the *embrace*, and where the lead is given and received, even when the dancers' chests are not actually touching. For the follower, the feeling is one of always seeking to re-establish that connection, to encircle the leader with her torso. I rather romantically view it as the physical expression of a longing to return to the shelter of the *embrace*. *Note:* As tango techniques and ways of understanding and describing them are highly individual, not all dancers will agree with this description. Consult your own personal teachers!

Embrace: The follower holds the leader's left hand with her right and places her left arm around his back, over his shoulder, holds either shoulder blade or (usually in an open embrace) takes hold of his upper right arm. Her left hand can be anywhere from his neck to his lower back. The leader encircles the follower with his right hand somewhere on the expanse of her back. Chests can be touching or not. Most dancers walk and perform simple moves in a close embrace, with chest contact, but they may open up the embrace to dance *giros* and other similar moves. In *milonguero* or *sustained close embrace* style, both sides of the follower's chest usually touch the leader's (the so-called "two-tit embrace"). In other styles, usually only the left-hand side makes contact (the "one-tit embrace"). There are no set hand or arm positions: it's a matter of personal preference and what feels comfortable for each couple. Ideally, the tango embrace should feel as warm, snugly and relaxed as a real-life embrace, while still permitting freedom of movement.

Encuentro milonguero: A weekend tango event, usually featuring several milongas, which may or may not include tango performances and classes, but which is centred on opportunities for social dancing. Like *tango marathons, encuentros* are usually gender balanced and, because of the limited numbers of dancers they can accommodate and their popularity, attendance at these events usually has to be booked in advance and participants are not always chosen on a first come-first served basis. *Encuentros* are generally differentiated from *marathons* by a strong preference for set seating at their milongas and a greater emphasis on the use of *cabeceo* and on *sustained close embrace* style.

Enrosque (lit. "spiral"): A movement which results in the feet wrapping around each other. Usually performed as a decoration by the leader when in the centre of a *giro*.

Fileteado: a type of artistic painting and lettering used in Buenos Aires with stylised flowing lines like the tendrils of plants. It is used to adorn all kind of beloved objects: signs, taxis, kioscos, and lorries. It was even used on the old *colectivos*.

Gancho (lit. "hook"): A move in which one dancer's leg hooks around the other's. This usually happens only when one dancer steps deep into the other's space. Some teachers believe the *gancho* does not need to be actively led, but should be performed whenever the relative positions of the legs comfortably allow it (which is surprisingly seldom). The move is not often seen in social *tango salón* and is illegal in the main *salón* competitions, but it is a frequent figure in *tango escenario* and in *salón* performances, too.

Giro (lit. "turn"): A turn in which, most commonly, the follower walks around the leader, who forms the centre of the turn. However, the leader can also walk around the follower or they can both walk around a common centre. Also sometimes called a *molinete*.

Lápiz (plural *lápices*) (lit. "pencil"): A decoration in which the free foot describes a circle on the floor.

Long-term beginners: My term for people who have been dancing tango for a long time, without significant improvement to the quality of their dance. This need not be a bad thing, except in the case of *toxic long-term beginners*.

Lunfardo: Buenos Aires slang, much of it drawn from Italian sources. The earlier tangos often have lyrics which are rich in colourful *lunfardo*. In 1943, the use of *lunfardo* was strongly discouraged in tango lyrics. Most tango lyrics from the 40s are written in standard Spanish.

Mate, also y*erba mate*, *Ilex paraguariensis*: A subtropical species of holly, drunk as a stimulant infusion at a temperature of around 80°C, which is very popular in Argentina and even more so in Uruguay. It is usually drunk from a gourd, using a metal straw (the *bombilla*). The *mate* gourd is passed from person to person, topped up from a thermos between drinkers by a *cebador* (person who serves *mate*). Everyone drinks from the same straw.

Milonga: 1. A tango dance event. 2. A style of music, related to tango, but with a dotted underlying rhythm and usually (though not always) a faster tempo. Tango itself is thought to have developed from this earlier form. Almost everyone who dances tango also dances *milonga*, though usually with slightly different choices of steps.

Milonguero/a: 1. A man or woman who frequents the *milongas*, usually an older person who has been doing so for many years. The word is often used as an honorific. 2. A style of dancing. See *tango milonguero*.

Mirada (lit. "look"): The practice of looking at someone in order to elicit an invitation to dance by *cabeceo* (q.v.).

Ocho: A *dissociated* turning step, performed by both leaders and followers, which is one of the most characteristic movements in tango. The name refers to the half figure eight pattern which the feet trace on the floor.

Orquesta Típica: The traditional tango orchestra, consisting of four bandoneons, four violins, piano and double bass. Tango music is usually categorised not by composer but by orchestra. The different orchestras have distinctive interpretive styles. Each orchestra is named for its conductor who may also be a member of the orchestra. So tangos "by Biagi" are tangos not written by Biagi but played by Rodolfo Biagi's orchestra. Biagi himself was their pianist. Many tangos are sung and it is customary to also identify the singer.

Tanturi-Campos, for example, is Ricardo Tanturi's orchestra accompanying the smooth tones of singer Enrique Campos, while Tanturi-Castillo features the rather nasal but strangely addictive voice of Alberto Castillo. At most *milongas*, it is not customary to announce which orchestra is playing, but experienced dancers recognise the characteristic sounds of most of the different orchestras that are usually played. Guessing the orchestra is also a favourite geeky game and the skill is often used as a marker of status.

Parada (lit. "stop"): In this movement, the follower is brought to a standstill, usually with at least one foot touching the leader's extended free foot, often with both dancers bending their knees and dipping down. It is frequently led at the end of a *giro*. Usually, the follower determines when to resume movement and the *parada* is a traditional place for the follower to add *adornos* or *decorations*.

Planeo: A movement performed by the leader, or led for the follower, which uses momentum to cause the free foot to describe a wide arc on the floor while the dancer turns. The two legs resemble a pair of compasses drawing a circle, with the free foot the pencil part.

Porteño/a: From the city of Buenos Aires (also called Capital Federal or CABA to differentiate it from densely populated Buenos Aires province, a separate legislative and electoral district).

Práctica: In theory, a more informal event than a *milonga* which provides a time and space for dancers to practise their steps, often under the watchful eye of a teacher. *Prácticas* typically do not use *cortinas* between *tandas*, so dancers can choose when to begin and end dancing at will. Actually, many so-called Buenos Aires *prácticas* are indistinguishable from informal *milongas*.

Ronda (lit. "circle"): The circle the dancers form on the floor during the dance. Tango is danced anticlockwise and couples usually progress within one or two circular lanes (with some dancers in the centre of the circle or circles). Changing between lanes, overtaking and tailgating are, ideally, kept to a minimum.

Rulo (lit. "curl"): A circular decoration executed by the leader or follower's free foot. I am not entirely sure of the difference, if any, between a *rulo* and a *lápiz* and regard them as roughly synonymous terms.

Sacada (lit. "displacement"): A move in which one partner deliberately invades the other's floor space, stepping close to or into the place their partner is currently occupying, thus displacing them. This often causes the partner's free leg to describe an arc along the floor. There may or may not be physical contact between the legs of the two partners at the moment of displacement.

Salida: A figure often danced as an opening to the dance, or to mark the beginning of a new phrase or section of the music. It characteristically begins with a side step, followed by some walking steps, and ends with the follower in what is called the cross, that is, with feet crossed left in front of right (with weight on the front foot). There are a number of different forms of *salida*. It is by no means compulsory to open the dance with a *salida* or, indeed, to dance one at any time, but some of the *salidas* are pleasing, well-designed and therefore popular figures. The *salida de los 40* is a personal favourite variant.

Slow Semite (the): My nickname for my tango partner, Aron Zvi Weiner. I chose it for its alliteration and in reference to the fact that Aron is Israeli and has a strong preference for slow music and a calm way of dancing.

Soltada (lit. "let go"): releasing the embrace to perform a move such as a turn.

Sustained close embrace: See *tango milonguero*.

Tanda (lit. "set"): At a *milonga*, the music is usually played in sets of three to five numbers, separated by a brief burst of non-tango music called the *cortina*, which is the tango equivalent of a palate cleanser at a wine tasting. The tracks in a *tanda* are almost always by the same orchestra, from the same period (if that orchestra spans various periods and styles) and, if they are sung tangos, with the same singer. Usually, dancers leave the floor during the *cortina* and often change partners at the start of the next *tanda*. At more traditional *milongas*, it is unusual to dance more than one consecutive *tanda* with the same person.

Tango diaspora: This is my own playful term for the tango world outside Buenos Aires.

Tango escenario, or stage tango: As the name suggests, a type of tango designed for stage shows, characterised by large, flashy movements. Often includes more acrobatic movements, lifts and jumps and sometimes fuses tango with other genres such as classical ballet and contemporary dance. Some movements have to be adapted to the rectangular space of the stage, since social tango is danced while travelling anticlockwise *around* a dance floor. Can also include a degree of histrionics ranging from the subtle to the camp. A very different style from the tango danced at the *milongas*. *Tango escenario* is typically choreographed, while the tango danced socially is improvised.

Tango marathon: These are weekend tango events, especially in Europe, the US or Canada, with *milongas* every night and frequently during the afternoons, too. To attend, dancers must book in advance for limited places and most *marathon* organizers ensure an equal number of leaders and followers. Many dancers are happy to travel to other cities in order to attend the local *marathons*, especially if there is a dearth of skilled dancers at their local *milongas*. The European *marathons* are said to have arisen in response to a felt need for more international dancing, a need which was not met by tango festivals, with their many workshops and classes and long evening performances. The first *marathons* took place at *El Corte* in Nijmegen, The Netherlands. This phenomenon is as yet unknown in Buenos Aires. See also *encuentro milonguero*.

Tango milonguero: A dance style in which the partners remain in a close embrace throughout the dance. It does not necessarily involve *apilado* and has nothing to do with being an old *milonguero* (not all *milongueros* dance this way). Some dancers prefer to describe this style of tango as *close embrace tango* or do not specifically differentiate it from other forms of *tango salón* (see the entry on *tango salón* below). Some people object strenuously to this name, which they see as borrowing prestige from the reputation of the old *milongueros* in a way that is inauthentic. Others dislike the name because they associate it with the well-known teacher Susana Miller, who was perhaps the first to popularise it and who is a controversial figure. As I dislike fighting over terminology (since *a rose by any other name would smell as sweet*), I prefer the more neutral and description term *sustained close embrace*.

Tango Nuevo: A dance style popularised by dancers Gustavo Naveira, Fabián Salas and Chicho Frumboli. It is characterised, typically, by extensive use of an open embrace and often by more elastic movements and a heavy landing on the beat. Certain steps, while they are also danced in other styles, are especially popular among *nuevo* dancers: particularly movements in which the follower is out of axis, with the dancers leaning towards each other (a *volcada*) or away from each other (a *colgada*). Many *nuevo* dancers, despite what the name might suggest, prefer to dance to traditional tango music from the 1940s or earlier. At the time of writing, *tango nuevo* is extremely unpopular and it is rare to see it danced here in Buenos Aires. Though I believe reports of its definitive death have been greatly exaggerated.

Tango Salón: A dance style in which the couple open and close the embrace fluidly in the course of the tango. One striking characteristic of *salón* is the preponderance of *giros*, turns in which the follower walks around the leader in an open embrace, while he turns on the spot, often embellishing his movement with decorations such as *enrosques* and *planeos*. Also often referred to as *Villa Urquiza style*. Some dancers prefer to use the expression in a more general sense to differentiate social dancing of a kind appropriate for the milonga from *tango escenario*.

Tangotonin: The hormonal neurotransmitter which dancers secrete in large quantities when enjoying a particularly wonderful dance. While scientists have as yet failed to identify its chemical structure or locate its receptors in the brain, empirical evidence demonstrates that its effects are powerful, dangerous and habit-forming.

Tango vals: Based on the Italian waltz, this is a style of tango music with a 3/4 beat (tango itself was traditionally written in 2/4 and is often called *dos por cuatro* for that reason). The dance itself is not significantly changed when dancing to this rhythm.

Technique practice: Solo exercises designed to enable dancers to incorporate and refine tango-specific ways of moving. The tango equivalent of ballet dancers' daily *barre* exercises.

Variación (variation): a fast musical passage, almost always played by the bandoneons, which provides the climax of many tangos.

Villa (pron. vee-zha) *Urquiza style*: See *tango salón*.

Volcada: See *tango nuevo*.

By The Same Author

The first volume of Our Tango World focusses on the learning experience and concludes with a guide to creating strong and healthy tango communities.

Terpsi believes passionately in learning and practice as the route not just to mastery of the dance, but to an ever-deepening world of pleasure and enjoyment. With her guidance, perhaps we can leave the *Land of the Long-Term Beginners* and gradually make our way towards the sunnier uplands of tango Elysium.

Our Tango World vol.1: Learning & Community

Released: 13 Dec 2018

ISBN: 978-1-9997551-8-8

About The Author

photo: Vanita Pune

Iona Italia started dancing tango more years ago then she cares to remember. In 2006 she decided to take an unpaid sabbatical from her life as an academic in the UK to improve her tango in Buenos Aires, thinking that she would return one year later as a tango goddess. Her illusions were shattered in her first private lesson, when her teacher stared at her in horror. Deciding to take her medicine, one year soon became ten.

In January 2011, she began her renowned blog "Tango Addiction" under the pseudonym Terpsichoral Tangoaddict, thinking of it more as an online diary. Soon she had thousands of readers.

Iona works as a freelance writer, editor and translator.

"Terpsi is tango's Everywoman" - Derrick Del Pilar